ST MARTIN'S
TRUE CRIME
CLASSICS

At 10:30 a.m. on Wednesday, March 1, Suzette sent Ahsa one final ICQ before she broke down her computer, which would then be put into storage. JR had just called to say he was on his way to the Guesthouse to drive her to the kennels to collect her dogs, as they were leaving first thing the following morning. But before they left he wanted to show her his farm, so they would later drive there with the dogs.

Ahsa teased Suzette about seeing the world with her new Master, saying she would have a great time.

"It will be fun, baby," wrote Suzette. "We all finally find what we want and need and I found mine."

While she was still online with Ahsa, JR arrived at the door to collect her.

"Well sweets I have to run," she wrote. "I'm off to the farm this morning for a while . . . grins . . . love to you baby."

That was the last time anyone would ever hear from Suzette . . . .

DEPRAVED

(Previously published as *Internet Slavemaster*)

JOHN GLATT

St. Martin's Paperbacks

Previously published under the title *Internet Slavemaster*.

DEPRAVED

Copyright © 2001 by John Glatt.

Cover photographs of John Robinson, Suzette Trouten, Catherine Clampitt, and Beverly Bonner courtesy AP/Wide World Photos.

ISBN: 0-312-93684-2
EAN: 80312-93684-6

Printed in the United States of America

St. Martin's Paperbacks edition / October 2001

10 9 8 7 6 5 4 3 2 1

ACKNOWLEDGMENTS

JOHN Edward Robinson Sr. will go down in criminal history as the first alleged serial killer to fully harness the power of the Internet to his perverted ends. Starting as a cheap con man in the mid-1960s, prosecutors say that Robinson soon progressed to multiple murder under the guise of "The Slavemaster," an inhuman sadist seeking out his hapless victims in bondage-and-domination–related Internet chat rooms.

Detectives now believe that the outwardly respectable fifty-seven-year-old Kansas grandfather may have killed up to nine women throughout the Midwest over his sixteen-year career. Even more incredibly he stands accused of murdering teenaged mother Lisa Stasi, just so her baby daughter Tiffany could be adopted by his own brother, an unwitting pawn in his demented scheme.

A month after his preliminary hearing in March 2001, the balding one-time businessman celebrated his thirty-seventh anniversary with his wife Nancy Jo, who has not been charged in any of the crimes. Friends say that Nancy and their four children do not recognize the man who is accused of murdering five women in cold blood and then stuffing their bodies in eighty-five-gallon oil barrels on his Kansas farm and in his storage locker in Missouri.

As a young boy John Robinson had wanted to become a priest, devoting himself to the pomp and ceremony of the Catholic Church. It was, he told everyone, his vocation. The struggle between good and evil had always been there, right at the very heart of the cherubic-looking lad, whom a teacher had once marked out as a future bishop. But somewhere the road had mysteriously forked, leading him into the darkest depths of evil and a unique place in criminal history, as America's alleged first Internet serial killer.

The "Internet Slavemaster Murders" took me deep into the twilight world of S&M where Robinson allegedly preyed on his victims. I would like to thank the slaves and masters who freely spoke to me off the record, providing invaluable background about the secret world they inhabit.

I am also indebted to many of the slaves who personally encountered "The Slavemaster" over the Internet and lived to tell me their stories. As a safety precaution, I have changed some of their names to protect them and their families, as there is still a stigma attached to the bondage lifestyle. Whenever names have been changed I have pointed this out in the book.

I would also like to thank Suzette Trouten's family and friends, who helped me reconstruct her last months and her fateful trip to Olathe to meet Robinson. Her mother Carolyn and sister Kim were especially generous to me, and her best friend Crystal Ferguson (not her real name) spent many hours being interviewed and guiding me through the hundreds of e-mails she'd received from "JT," "JR," and other aliases allegedly used by John Robinson.

I would also like to thank my generous hosts in Kansas City, Steve Treaster and Toni Wood, who not only showed me the city they love but proved invaluable by helping me monitor the progress of the case. Thanks must also go to: Betsy Phillips, Editor of the *Democrat Missourian*, for her razor-sharp insight and guidance; Kevin Petrehn of KSHB-TV; and Sergeant Rick Roth of the Lenexa Police Department.

I am also indebted to Johnson County District Attorney Paul Morrison and Cass County District Attorney Chris Koster for all their help. Gratitude also goes to: Jim, Margaret and Hilary Adams, Josephine Bermel, Todd Bond of the Johnson County Library, Dr. William Bonner, Bonnie Brooks, Richard Clinton, Randy Davis, Scott Davis, Bill Godfrey, Dr. Bruce Graham, Steve Gwartney, Marianne Horton, Bruce Houdek, Layne Hudson, Sara Khan, David Klinginsmith, James Krcmarik, Russell Krebs, Sharon LaPrad, Robert Meyers of Friendley's Bookstore, Kathy Muttocks, Eugenia Reece, Paul Reiff, Henry Robinson, Thomas Kelly Ryan, Carlos Santiago, April Shepard, Phil Spell, Carl Stasi, Sandy Steckly, John Tinsley, Ron Wood and all the staff at Extended Stay America in Overland Park, Kansas.

As always I would like to thank my editor at St. Martin's Press, Charles Spicer, and his team, Joseph Cleemann and Anderson Bailey, and my agent, Peter Miller and his staff at PMA. Special thanks goes to PMA's Delin Cormeny, who grew up in Olathe and provided me with my initial key contacts.

Thanks also to: Wensley Clarkson, Annette Witheridge, Roger Hitts, Daphna Inbar, Danny and Allie Trachtenberg, Cari Pokrassa and Susan Chenery.

CONTENTS

DEPRAVED

PROLOGUE

SUMMER had come early to Kansas. By 9:00 a.m. on Memorial Day, 2000, temperatures were already in the eighties and would peak at ninety-two degrees. It was the prelude to an unrelenting heat wave, which would claim many lives in one of the hottest Kansas summers on record.

There were few people out in the hazy early morning sunshine in Olathe, the prim, proper Johnson County seat of government, situated twenty miles south of Kansas City off I-35, which slices through Kansas and Missouri like a knife. And there was hardly any traffic as the full-sized Dodge pick-up careered around the off-ramp from I-35 to turn right onto Sante Fe, Olathe's main commercial artery of shabby strip malls and fast-food restaurants.

Although most people were looking forward to a quiet, leisurely Memorial Day with their families, John Edward Robinson Sr. had more weighty matters on his mind. The bespectacled 56-year-old grandfather had to keep up appearances. As usual he would attend his own annual barbecue, a tradition on the Santa Barbara Estates, which was managed by his wife, Nancy Jo. But he would merely be going through the motions, making small talk and being gregarious.

For John Robinson was under siege. An elite squad of detectives and FBI agents believed him to be one of the most prolific serial murderers at large in America. And they were closing in for the kill. Indeed some primitive animal instinct told Robinson that his days of freedom were numbered. But why should it spoil his traditional Memorial Day celebrations? It would be a challenge to show the detectives that he had the upper hand. They were playing out of their league and he would outsmart them, as he always had in the past.

Robinson favored a Western macho look, wearing denim jeans and cowboy hats or, when it suited his purpose, preppy golf attire. His warm, winning smile had fooled many people over the years. At first it appeared charming, but on closer inspection it revealed a deep streak of arrogant superiority, just beneath the surface.

Robinson's many lives were assiduously compartmentalized, like the perfect filing systems he had once designed during his days running his own businesses. He had turned dissembling into an art form, constructing a crazed patchwork quilt of personas. But recently things had not gone according to plan.

Over the last few weeks he had sensed *them* getting closer and closer. Ironic, he would think, this new feeling of pursuit.

To family, friends and neighbors he was a mild-mannered, one-time entrepreneur, at present down on his luck, who could always be counted on for a helping hand. Once active in the local scouts and various sporting associations, he was proud of his civic accomplishments and loved to boast about them at any opportunity.

But in the underground world of bondage, domination and sadomasochism (BDSM), police say he was "The Slavemaster," a supreme master's master of the black arts of torture and whipping. No depths of depravity would satisfy him.

He had spent a long night on his computer and felt weary, as he drew up outside the Price Chopper supermarket on Sante Fe, to buy hot dogs, hamburgers and charcoal briquettes. But his thoughts were apparently on less mundane matters, because, as several women would later testify, he was finalizing plans to bring more playmates to Kansas City over the summer. Like all the others, they would happily fly across the country to satisfy their craving for bondage at his experienced hands.

The immaculately laid-out Santa Barbara Estates models itself on a Southern California–style resort, boasting street names like Palo Alto, Pasadena, Palm Springs and Monterrey Lane—where the Robinsons lived at #36. Nancy Robinson had been managing the upscale trailer park for five years, soon establishing a stern reputation, alienating some of the residents with her aggressive behavior.

Her husband John kept a far lower profile, mostly staying inside their smart double-trailer or doing odd jobs around the estate. If he wasn't out working on his garden, he would spend his days in his trailer office on the computer, the shades always drawn. When anyone asked what he was doing, he would explain that he was setting up a new Website for the mobile home community.

But exactly what he did for a living remained a mystery. The Robinsons lived well, with a farm in the country, several cars and a truck, even the occasional foreign vacation. Every Christmas and Halloween Robinson spent hours festively decorating his prized garden and the outside of his trailer. One year he had even dressed up as Santa Claus for the Santa Barbara kids.

But there was an undercurrent of gossip about him on the estate. It was said that he had propositioned several female neighbors, and one thirteen-year-old girl would later claim that the balding Robinson had made "creepy" remarks of a sexual nature to her.

By early afternoon John was hard at work setting up

the barbecue at the side of the swimming pool next to his wife's office. The pool was the social hub of the estate, with its reclining beach chairs and umbrellas that gave it the look of a luxury hotel.

John Robinson seemed in a particularly jovial mood, wearing a golf shirt over his growing paunch, and tight swimming trunks. Some would later remember him as the life and soul of the barbecue, cracking jokes as he prepared an endless stream of chicken wings, hot dogs and hamburgers.

Even the detectives, watching his every move through long-range cameras, were secretly impressed by his coolness. They wondered whether he'd be quite so happy when they soon moved in to arrest him.

But as the sun beat down through the gathering clouds, Robinson didn't appear to have a care in the world, outside of burning the hamburgers.

CHAPTER I

BY ROYAL COMMAND

JOHN Edward Robinson was born on December 27, 1943, in the Chicago suburb of Cicero, Illinois, the third of five children. His father, Henry Robinson Sr., worked as a machinist for Western Electric and his mother Alberta was a homemaker, bringing up John, his elder brother Henry Jr., younger brother Donald and sisters Jo Ann and Mary Ellen. The Robinsons were a typical family in Cicero, a largely blue-collar neighborhood on the western border of Chicago.

Cicero has a long and distinguished tradition of crime, dating back to the Civil War. Bribery and corruption had always been rife among police officials and politicians, who aligned themselves with criminals and prospered from rum-selling, robbery and prostitution.

"The human scum of a hundred cities swarmed [in] from all over the country," noted local historian, Herb Asbury.

Cicero became world-famous as the headquarters of legendary gangster Al Capone, who ran his criminal empire from the old Hawthorne Arms Hotel on 22nd Street, just a few blocks away from where John Robinson was born.

Brooklyn-bred "Scarface" Capone was first drafted into Chicago in 1919 by underworld boss Johnny Torrio, to help run the rackets. A year later came Prohibition and, operating out of Cicero, Capone turned illegal alcohol into a multi-million-dollar business. It took Capone just five years to transform Chicago into the crime capital of America, with a chain of speakeasies, supplying willing patrons around the clock with prostitutes, gambling, illegal whiskey and beer.

In 1924, when Henry Robinson Sr. was eight years old, police chased Al Capone down Cicero Avenue, killing his brother Frank in a hail of bullets. A year later Capone hit back when the body of Assistant State's Attorney General William H. McSwiggin was found dumped on a Cicero street.

Capone's infamous Hawthorne Inn fortress had steel-shuttered windows, electronically operated doors and squads of fully-armed sentries. It would become the blueprint for all mob hideouts in the newly popular gangster movies that John Robinson loved as a young boy.

Al Capone's reign finally ended when he was found guilty of tax evasion and sent to Alcatraz. On his release in November 1939 he moved to a secluded Florida estate, where he died a broken man seven years later of paresis, a brain-destroying disease caused by syphilis.

As John Robinson grew up, his parents would capture his vivid imagination with their own thrilling recollections of Capone and the Chicago gang. The Mafia and corruption were still part of everyday life in Cicero, and as a small boy John set his sights on becoming a gangster if the priesthood didn't pan out.

Most hard-working Cicero residents liked the Mafia, which was seen as reassuring insurance against street crime by outsiders. The general feeling was that the gangsters were good to the kids and only hurt their own kind.

It was a staunchly working-class town with corner bars and elm tree–lined streets, where men carried lunch pails to work and returned home at 5:00 p.m. after a hard day to find their dinner on the table. Years later John Robinson would tell a Kansas Department of Corrections psychiatrist that his father was a binge-drinker who left it to Alberta to discipline the children.

At the heart of Cicero was the Sportsman Park Race-track, which drew gamblers and drinkers from all over Chicago. The monotonous strains of the track announcer on the public address system could be heard blocks away, and became part of Cicero folklore.

Growing up in the post-war years, John Robinson knew the streets of Cicero well, often walking past Capone's now-faded Hawthorne Hotel. His father worked nearby at the Western Electric Company's Hawthorne Works, its huge towering smokestacks belching thick black smoke into the sky, often obscuring the sun.

It was a bleak, depressing place to grow up in and there were few opportunities for an ambitious boy like John Robinson to break out into the world outside.

One escape was the Boy Scouts and his father, who was active in the Chicago scouting scene, encouraged the twelve-year-old to join Pack 259, which was sponsored by the Holy Name Society of Mary Queen of Heaven Roman Catholic Church.

"There wasn't much to do in Cicero," said James Krcmarik, who belonged to the same scout group. "Scouts were the way out for us to get swimming, canoeing and the outdoors."

Krcmarik remembers John Robinson as a "weedy little guy" who was "quiet and nondescript." He was a loner with few friends but already felt superior to everyone else and was not afraid to tell them so.

In the fall of 1957, the cherubic-faced Robinson seemed to live up to his boasts when he was accepted at the prestigious Quigley Preparatory Seminary. The *Chicago Tribune* even reported the story, citing his "scholastic ability, scouting experience and poise." This was quite an achievement for a working-class Cicero boy and the Robinson family was very proud.

The Quigley Seminary was in the very center of downtown Chicago and resembled an imposing gothic cathedral. Just a stone's throw away from the landmark Water Tower, it was founded in 1905 by Archbishop James E. Quigley with a mission to educate the city's future priests. It would later become one of the top schools of its kind in America.

In the beginning there were just fifty-two high school freshmen, but by the mid-fifties when Robinson enrolled, the student body had grown to over 1300. Plans were already underway to enlarge it even further with a new high school, which was finally completed in 1961.

The seminary provided a five-year course for young Catholic boys looking for a good education before joining the priesthood. Robinson often spoke of having a true vocation, saying that one day he wanted to serve the Vatican. Even as a boy John Robinson had a silver tongue and could argue convincingly about anything.

On November 3, 1957, Robinson, who was senior patrol leader of his troop, was named an Eagle Scout along with James Krcmarik—the only two Cicero scouts to attain this ultimate scouting achievement. To make Eagle, both boys had had to pass a total of twenty merit badges, including mandatory ones in nature, first aid, swimming, lifesaving, canoeing and rowing.

There was a big ceremony for the new Eagle Scouts at the J. Sterling Morton High School in Cicero, which was attended by John Robinson's proud parents. Making the presentation, Leland D. Cornell, scout executive of the Chicago Boy Scout Council, told the 126 new Eagle Scouts, from all over the Chicago area, that they were "elite" future leaders.

"The kind of a city that Chicago will be is in your hands," he declared. "It can be beautiful or ugly, clean or filthy, honest or corrupt."

After the ceremony John Robinson proudly showed off his Eagle Scout badge to everybody and even upset some by his immodesty.

"He was bragging to everyone that he was the youngest guy ever made Eagle Scout," remembers Krcmarik. "I said, 'That's fine, buddy. I don't really care.' "

Two weeks later John Robinson flew to London and led 120 boy scouts onto the stage of the London Palladium to perform for the Queen of England in a Royal Command Performance. How he had come to be chosen as the sole American scout representative in the annual Ralph Reader Gang Show remains a mystery. But the event made the front page of the *Chicago Tribune* on November 19, 1957, under the headline "Chicago Boy Scout Leads Troop to Sing for Queen."

According to the article, Robinson, who was lauded as the youngest American ever to perform at the world-famous home of London vaudeville, was extremely cocky. He even traded jokes before the show with fellow performer Judy Garland in her dressing room.

"We Americans gotta stick together," Robinson told the superstar.

"You're right," said the delighted Garland, giving him a big kiss on the cheek.

He also charmed legendary English actress and singer Gracie Fields during rehearsals, and she took the smiling scout from Cicero under her wing.

"You're a mighty handsome youngster," she told him. And to the amusement of *Chicago Tribune* reporter Arthur Veysey, Robinson instantly agreed with her.

When Gracie Fields asked if he planned to visit Italy, where she lived on the Isle of Capri, off the coast of Naples, he replied that he planned to study for the priesthood after he graduated Quigley, and would then come to Rome. Scooping the little boy up in her arms for a hug, Fields extended an open invitation for him to visit her anytime.

Then, as the London Palladium curtain went up, John Robinson, wearing a bright scarlet uniform, led the scouting ensemble onto the stage, as Queen Elizabeth applauded enthusiastically from her royal box. He then bowed and sang a special tribute to the Queen, as the sole American scout in the show: "You are the emblem of our flag, red, white and blue."

After the show the young American was asked by reporters if he had been nervous, appearing in front of the Queen and meeting Judy Garland.

"I wasn't scared," he declared, "but I was surprised, all right."

For the next four days he was feted as an ambassador of American scouting, staying at the home of an English scout and getting a guided tour of London.

Ironically, John Robinson's first-ever appearance on the front page of a newspaper was alongside the gruesome story of infamous Chicago serial murderer and self-confessed cannibal Ed Gein, who ate the body of one female victim and was suspected of killing at least ten others at his farm in Plainfield, Illinois.

John Robinson's brush with greatness was brief, as were his aspirations for the priesthood. The rest of his school days at Quigley were undistinguished and he was seen as an average student. In 1958, at the age of fourteen, he appeared in the Quigley Seminary yearbook, *Le Petit Seminaire*. But although he looked like an angelic altar boy, his dark hair cropped short over the ears, he wore a sly, enigmatic smile, like one of the alien children in the science fiction movie *Village of the Damned*. This would be his only appearance in the Quigley yearbook.

Richard Shotke, former public relations director of the

Chicago Boy Scouts, still remembers Robinson as an above-average student, "not brilliant" but already cunningly manipulative.

"[He was] a good kid," Shotke recalled. "He didn't talk a great deal, but when he did talk, it was to produce an effect that he wanted. He was shrewd."

In his late teens John Robinson visited Canada on a boy scouts' singing tour. After one performance he met a pretty young girl named Mary White (not her real name), who was four years younger than him. The two teenagers started talking after the show. They discovered that they had a lot in common, and exchanged addresses. On his return to Chicago, Robinson and Mary became pen pals, regularly exchanging letters over the next several years, becoming life-long friends.

In 1961 Robinson finally graduated at the age of seventeen with average grades, doing well in science but not in math. He had given up the idea of becoming a priest, enrolling in Morton Junior College in Cicero to prepare himself for a future career.

Opened in 1924, at the height of the Al Capone era, Morton Community College helped pioneer the community college movement, which aimed to make inexpensive high-quality education available to everybody. It taught a general education course up to a bachelor's degree to students who couldn't afford four years' college tuition.

With five children to feed, Henry Robinson's machinist job at Western Electric left little money for the luxury of education. So after his son John's disappointment at Quigley, he was given one final chance at Morton, where he trained to be an X-ray technician at the college's continuing education program.

With his usual delusions of grandeur, John Robinson now determined to become a doctor. Although he was a poor student, dropping out of Morton after just two years with no qualifications, he resolved not to let that stand in the way of the distinguished medical career he now envisaged.

Over the next few years he would continually lie about his qualifications, claiming to have received his medical training at West Suburban Hospital in Oak Park Hill, Illinois. He would even proudly display elaborately framed degree certificates on his office walls at several medical establishments he tricked into employing him. But West Suburban Hospital officials have no records of ever certifying Robinson, or indicating that he ever registered with their state licensing board.

In 1964, at the age of twenty-one, John Robinson married a local Chicago girl named Nancy Jo Lynch. The twenty-year-old attractive willowy blonde had fallen for the smooth-talking X-ray technician, who was now working in a Chicago hospital. When the tall, boyish-looking Robinson proposed on one of their first dates, she accepted. Before long she was pregnant with his child.

They married in a Cicero church at a Catholic ceremony attended by both slightly embarrassed families. Henry and Alberta Robinson now hoped their troubled son would finally settle down and meet his new responsibilities with a wife and a baby on the way.

But within months Robinson was in trouble, suspected of embezzling money from the hospital where he was working. He finally agreed to repay the money in full on the understanding that his bosses did not go to the police.

John and Nancy now left Chicago under a cloud. It was whispered that he had been a low-rung member of the Chicago mob since he was a teenager and involved in many illegal rackets. Eventually, said the gossip, he had been caught stealing from one of the bosses and fled with his now-heavily-pregnant wife, fearing for his life.

Years later Robinson would boast to friends that he had been run out of Chicago by the mob, hinting that there had been a contract out on his life. It would be several years before he set foot in Chicago again.

CHAPTER 2

AN APPRENTICESHIP IN CRIME

JOHN and Nancy Robinson headed west to Kansas City in late 1964, joining the rush of ambitious young couples settling in Johnson County, Kansas, a bedroom community just south of the city. The endless acres of lush green farmlands had hardly changed since the Civil War, when the area was known as a grazing spot for pack animals.

In the mid-1800s Kansas City stood as the westernmost border of the United States with little but free-roaming Indian tribes between there and California. It was wild, frontier country at the very edge of civilization.

The legendary twelve-hundred-mile Sante Fe Trail—a trade pipeline funneling silver, furs and other goods through five states between Missouri and Mexico—plowed right through the center of Johnson County. Then the crossroads of America, the trail would play a vital role in the westward expansion of the United States and make Kansas City one of the richest cities in the nation.

Even today it is easy to imagine the trail riders loading up the wagon trains and setting off from Kansas City across the prairie to conquer the unknown West. Later came the transcontinental railway, which used Kansas City as a jumping-off point during the 1849 California Gold Rush.

Legends of the old wild West like Jesse and Frank James and Bloody Bill Anderson lived on the Missouri side of the Missouri River, pitting their wits and guns against lawmen like Buffalo Bill Cody and Wild Bill Hickok, on the Kansas side.

The borderline which divides Kansas and Missouri ploughs down from where the Kansas and Missouri Rivers meet in the center of Kansas City. Then it goes south along today's State Line Road.

There is still an uneasy truce between the two states that harks back to the Civil War and the many atrocities committed between the Confederate and Union soldiers. Even today all the Lawrence-based University of Kansas sports teams are nicknamed the Jayhawks, after the Kansas pro-abolitionist Jayhawkers, who murdered, looted and pillaged across the border in Missouri during the Civil War. The rival teams from the University of Missouri in Columbia are the Tigers, adopted from a Union home guard unit that was the last line of defense against the Jayhawkers.

Today many people from Kansas cross state lines twice a day to work in Missouri and vice-versa. And Missouri housewives think nothing of crossing the border into Kansas to shop at their favorite malls.

Indeed there are two distinctly separate Kansas Cities: one lying on the westernmost edge of Missouri and the other on the eastern tip of Kansas. The local television stations differentiate them by referring to one as KCK and the other KCMO. Tourists are easily confused but get used to the lay of the land after a few days.

KCMO is three times as big as its smaller sister, KCK. It is a center of the arts with its renowned opera and ballet companies and luxury malls. The beautiful art deco Country Club Plaza, built by J. C. Nichols in 1922 and modeled after Seville in Spain, has recently been restored to its former glory. It is a shoppers' paradise with its upscale boutiques and fine restaurants. In comparison KCK is a shabbily poor second cousin that has always struggled to survive.

When John and Nancy Robinson arrived in the mid-1960s Johnson County was still largely a rural area. It would be another few years before the great expansion that would turn the county into one of the most affluent in America. At that time there were no huge malls or upscale housing and Johnson County was a place of beautifully quaint wooden houses with front porches and miles and miles of uninterrupted farmland.

But things were about to change dramatically, and as soon as he arrived the ever-opportunistic John Robinson knew he was in the right place at the right time to reap the benefits.

Soon after arriving John Robinson interviewed for a job as a pediatric X-ray technician at Children's Mercy and General Hospitals on Main Street. He told Dr. Charles Shopfner, a professor of radiology at the University of Missouri, that he had just been accepted in medical school to become a doctor and needed a night job to finance his day classes. He even produced certificates and letters of recommendation from Morton College stating that he was a trained radiographic technologist, nuclear medical technologist and medical lab technologist.

"The doctor was completely taken in by this young man, as were the rest of us," remembers Josephine Bermel, who worked with Robinson at Mercy Hospital. "I thought, Wow, he's young and very bright and is going to be a doctor. He was very personable and easy to like."

But once on the job it was soon obvious that Robinson was a clumsy technician and knew little about taking X-rays. Initially Bermel gave him the benefit of the doubt, thinking that perhaps the problem was that he had never worked with children before.

"He started working as the night technician at Mercy and he really wasn't very good," she explains. "[Children] don't understand when you say, 'Take a deep breath.' And positioning is very important and the machinery is intimidating. We had to teach him how to do it."

In January 1965, Nancy Jo made John Robinson a father for the first time when she gave birth to a baby boy they named John Jr. But at just twenty-one, Robinson had no intention of being a faithful husband and father. Most nights he would go out carousing around the shady bars and clubs of downtown Kansas City looking for thrills and excitement. There was soon gossip at the hospital that he entertained several girlfriends while Nancy stayed in their apartment looking after their newborn son.

Jo Bermel heard these stories from an X-ray company worker, who socialized with Robinson and felt sorry for his young wife.

"It was kind of a sordid tale," she remembers. "Here was a young married man with a family, and he had a girlfriend that he was supposed to be supporting. At the time I was thinking, How could he get himself so terribly mixed up like this? He really was an enigma."

It wasn't long before Dr. Shopfner began to "get wise" to Robinson and after several warnings fired him. But on April 1, 1966, he landed an even better job at the Fountain Plaza X-Ray Laboratory, owned by President Harry S Truman's personal physician, Dr. Wallace H. Graham.

A decorated World War II hero and former Golden Gloves boxing champion, Dr. Graham was a successful general surgeon who had a thriving practice and X-ray laboratory at 1815 E. 63rd Street.

At his interview in Dr. Graham's upstairs medical office, the smooth-talking Robinson was full of enthusiasm and oozed confidence. Dr. Wallace, a former Eagle Scout himself, was well-impressed with the ambitious young man and hired him on the spot to run his laboratory and X-ray department.

"He had all these big ideas," says Dr. Graham's son Dr. Bruce Graham, who worked under Robinson as a fifteen-year-old summer intern and now runs his late father's practice. "I never really liked him or trusted him. I thought he was creepy."

Delighted with his new, well-paying executive job, John Robinson immediately put up half-a-dozen medical diplomas on his office wall, purporting to have come from various prestigious medical establishments around Illinois.

But Robinson seemed lazy, delegating most of his duties to his small staff. Bruce Graham found himself doing most of the work while Robinson came up with dynamic new schemes to streamline the office.

Soon after joining Fountain Plaza, Robinson became a father again when Nancy Jo gave birth to a baby girl they named Kimberly. He proudly brought in photographs of his beautiful new baby to show the staff. But again Robinson found himself the subject of much gossip for his erratic and strange behavior both in and out of the office.

It was said that he seduced female patients in the X-ray laboratory, telling one in particular that his wife was terminally ill. He also "shocked" Dr. Graham's teenage son by boasting of his sexual conquests and the double life he led by night in the seedier clubs of Kansas City.

"He'd talk about a lot of weird sexual things," remembers Bruce Graham. "I was a fifteen-year-old guy and he's telling me about this place he went called the Jewel Box, where they had male transvestites. He thought that was big fun but I thought it was really strange."

That Christmas the busy practice started losing money for no apparent reason. Things became so bad that Dr. Graham couldn't even afford to pay the staff their annual holiday bonuses. But as the rest of the office despaired, fearing that they might soon be laid off, John Robinson was thriving. Totally insensitive to the current pessimistic office atmosphere, he would frequently boast about buying choice lake-front property, a new car for Nancy, and dogs and horses.

Dr. Graham's partner Philip Reister was suspicious of Robinson, often criticizing the poor quality of his work. Reister thought that Dr. Graham's golden boy worked far too fast to carry out accurate testing, citing an example of how he had once poured a patient's urine sample down the sink by mistake.

So to curry favor and save his job, Robinson walked into Reister's office one day and presented him with a baby poodle as a gift for his family.

Six months later a bookkeeper discovered that John Robinson had embezzled more than $100,000 from Fountain Plaza X-Ray, using Dr. Graham's signature stamp to process checks and cash them for his own benefit. He also had patients by-pass the billing counter and write their checks directly out to him.

Dr. Graham was shocked and disappointed when he heard this, calling Robinson into his office to explain himself. Robinson was completely unruffled, coolly replying that he had merely "transferred funds," and offering to pay back the money he had stolen.

Dr. Graham refused the offer and called the police.

As they were waiting for them to arrive, he asked Robinson how he had ever thought he would get away with it. Robinson then admitted he knew he would be caught eventually but was otherwise unapologetic. Dr. Graham Sr. would later ponder "how such a young fellow like him could get into such a scrape."

When the Kansas police arrived they immediately arrested Robinson, escorting him out of the medical office in handcuffs.

"We were all fooled," said Dr. Bruce Graham, who believes Robinson stole at least three times the amount he was charged with taking. "There was so much money that we could never track."

Later it was discovered that Robinson had even stolen one of the office chairs.

In August 1969, John Robinson was convicted by a Johnson County jury of embezzling $33,000 from Fountain X-Ray. He received a suspended sentence and was put on three years probation.

Nancy Robinson attended his trial at the Johnson County Courthouse in Olathe with her two young children, taking the stand as a character witness for her husband. No one who was in court that day didn't feel sorry for the young, pretty blonde-haired mother.

"She was a meek, soft-spoken lady," remembers Dr. Bruce Graham, who was at the court hearing. "She was telling everyone what a good guy he was."

Soon after he was fired Josephine Bermel answered an advertisement in *The Kansas City Star* for John Robinson's old job, unaware that she would be replacing her former Mercy Hospital colleague.

She got the job and on her first day she moved into John Robinson's office and noticed the impressive array of medical diplomas lining the walls.

"When I finally found out John Robinson had worked

there I thought, 'My God, I don't think he's had all this schooling,' " she said.

A few weeks later Bermel was cleaning the X-ray darkroom when she discovered a case full of hundreds of blank certificates wrapped in cellophane, which Robinson had not had time to remove when he was arrested.

"It was unbelievable," said Bermel. "I went upstairs and told Dr. Graham what I had found. I think his remark was, 'Well, you know, Jo, I was really wondering just how young he was when he started school because he had so many [qualifications].' "

At the age of twenty-five, Robinson now officially had a criminal record and had launched his career as a petty thief and con man.

John Robinson now set his sights on the corporate world, joining the Kansas City, Missouri, branch of Mobil Oil as a systems analyst. Once again he used forged references to talk his way into the job, neglecting to mention that he was on probation.

Before long his dishonesty caught up with him again in September 1970, when he was caught stealing 372 dollars' worth of postage stamps. Three months later he worked out a deal with the courts to pay back full restitution. The charge was reduced to a misdemeanor.

Soon afterwards John and Nancy Robinson decided to move back to Chicago, where he found work as an insurance salesman for the R. B. Jones Company. But leaving Kansas City breached the conditions of his three-year probation, as he had neglected to tell his probation officer that he was moving to take a new job.

The smooth-talking young con man seemed to have found his niche selling insurance around the Chicago area, soon impressing his new bosses with his success. But once again he couldn't resist stealing. This time he was caught red-handed embezzling $5,586.36 from R. B. Jones and the police were called in.

Robinson readily admitted the theft and got off lightly when the Illinois state attorney agreed to dismiss the case, after Robinson paid restitution. But as a matter of course the Chicago court reported the matter to the Jackson County Circuit Court in Kansas. Robinson was immediately ordered back to the state, where a circuit court judge extended his three-year probation.

CHAPTER 3

MAN OF THE YEAR

In early 1971, in the midst of her husband's latest legal troubles, Nancy Robinson became pregnant again. Later that year she gave birth to a set of beautiful blonde fraternal twins they named Christopher and Christine, who would complete the Robinson family.

Although John Robinson had never been faithful, Nancy apparently had no idea of his numerous affairs. She always believed his stories of working late, as he caroused in the downtown bars looking for sex. If he was a con man at work, he was an even bigger one at home.

Friends of the couple pitied the nervous, chain-smoking young mother who had always remained loyal, despite all his run-ins with the law. It would be ten years before she finally took a stand against him.

Now back in Kansas City, John Robinson decided to go into business for himself. He moved his growing family into a house at 1514 Orchard Road in Raytown, Missouri, and established a medical consulting company called Professional Services Association, Inc. He then hired a pretty 24-year-old secretary named Charlotte Bowersock at seven dollars an hour, taking office space at 9503 East 63rd Street, in Raytown.

"I was literally paid to keep my mouth shut," remembers Bowersock, who was five months pregnant when Robinson hired her. Over the next few months Robinson would often give Bowersock handwritten scripts to type onto faked letterheads before he would sign the forgeries. Once when she questioned him about his unusual business methods, he assured her that the people whose names he was forging were friends of his and he was doing them a favor, as they were too busy to write the letters themselves.

Today Bowersock admits to being "naïve as all get-out," turning a blind eye to her former boss's unethical practices as she didn't want to lose the well-paying job.

As president of his new company the young entrepreneur bought a smart new car and several business suits, so he could look the part of a successful businessman and impress would-be clients. Before long the University of Kansas Medical Center hired him as a business consultant for its Family Practice Department.

At his screening interview the departmental chairman, Jack Walker, who was also the Mayor of Overland Park, was so impressed with John Robinson that he brought him into a staff meeting, which voted him straight onto the payroll.

"He came and presented himself to me as an expert as a physicians' professional consultant," Walker would tell *The Kansas City Star* some years later. "He made a very good impression: well-dressed, nice-looking, late twenties, seemed to know a lot, very glib, good speaker."

But within a few months, Robinson was in trouble after doctors at the Medical Center's orthopedic surgery department, which was also using Professional Services Association, started having "doubts about his handling" of its financial affairs.

Then Robinson called Jack Walker, requesting the corporation's checkbook. The bookkeeper, who was already suspicious of Robinson, refused to hand it over. Finally Walker stepped in and, after learning other "troubling" information regarding Robinson's business practices, let him go.

Robinson now concentrated on pursuing potential investors to inject some new capital into his company. Calling on his talents as a forger, he faked two letters designed to put Professional Services Association on the local business map and make him a rich man. Unfortunately for Robinson his latest ambitious con was also one of his least successful.

To first improve his professional status in the medical community, Robinson called Charlotte Bowersock into his office and dictated a letter to himself, from the Board of Regents at the University of Missouri. It would inform him that the board had just made him a full professor, along with its rights and privileges. At the bottom he forged the signature of Dean Hamilton B. G. Robinson of the University of Missouri, Kansas City, School of Dentistry.

Unfortunately the University did not have a "Board of Regents," and the dean's name and signature—which bore an uncanny resemblance to his own—were forgeries.

Then Robinson forged another outrageous letter, which would ultimately lead to a four-count grand jury indictment for security and mail fraud.

After John Hartlein, the group executive director of the prestigious Kansas-based Marion Laboratories, turned down his request to invest in PSA, an undaunted Robinson dictated a letter to himself from the pharmaceutical distributor, saying it wanted to take over his company.

The new PSA prospectus, which was sent out to potential common stock investors on November 19, 1973, carried the letter bearing Hartlein's bogus signature and mentioning Marion Laboratory Founder Ewing W. Kauffman. It claimed that Professional Services Association was presently a take-over target for the multi-million-dollar publicly owned company listed on the New York Stock Exchange. Anyone with this insider information who was to invest in PSA stock could make a financial killing. The forgery read:

> Dear Mr. Robinson:
>   At Mr. Kaufman's [sic] request, I have received the material you submitted on November 15th, 1973. It is the decision of the executive committee that we continue discussions toward making Professional Services Association, Inc., a wholly owned subsidiary of Marion Laboratories, Inc.
>   We will begin discussions for your training manuals at $364,000. Of course, you will be a necessary part of our overall plan, if we can reach an agreement in the near future.
>   If you have any questions, please do not hesitate to contact me.
>
>   Yours very truly,
>   S/John E. Hartlin/[sic]
>   John E. Hartlein
>   Group Executive

The letter was riddled with mistakes. Robinson misspelled Hartlein's signature, omitting an 'e,' and also managed to get the name of the founder of Marion Laboratory, Ewing M. Kauffman, wrong. After sending out the prospectus to a list of prospective investors, Robinson sat back and waited for the calls to come in.

When Prairie Village businessman Mac F. Cahal received the letter, he called Robinson and was sent a balance sheet vastly inflating the value of PSA's "training and reference manuals," which were the company's sole assets.

Unfortunately for Robinson, Cahal also happened to

be friends with Ewing Kauffman and called him after sending off a $2,500 down payment for ten thousand stocks of PSA at a dollar each. The next day Kauffman called Cahal, and "hit the ceiling" when he heard about the letter with his fake signature. Cahal immediately stopped his check and called in the U.S. Securities and Exchange Commission, which began an investigation into John Robinson and his PSA company.

On December 10, 1975, a federal grand jury in Missouri returned a four-count indictment against Robinson for securities fraud, mail fraud and for falsely misrepresenting PSA. His secretary Charlotte Bowerstock was never charged.

On May 24, 1976, John Robinson pleaded no contest to the charges of interstate securities fraud. Three weeks later U.S. District Court Judge John W. Oliver fined him $2,500 and placed him on a further three years' probation. The Securities and Exchange Commission also ordered Robinson not to defraud any investors in the future, or face far more serious contempt of court charges.

Robinson's lawyer, Bruce Houdek, said they deliberately pleaded no contest to avoid him having to pay back the money he had taken from his stockholders.

"We didn't want to expose [Robinson] to automatic liability," said Houdek. "The judge permitted us to do this. It's a legal tactic for his benefit."

Reflecting on his former client, Houdek would later describe him as "a small-time, penny-ante con guy" who "worked harder getting out of trouble than getting into it."

Although his conviction, with the subsequent publicity in *The Kansas City Star*, looked like the end of Robinson's career in business, he would soon bounce back with a slew of even more audacious scams.

* * *

In July 1977, John Robinson moved his wife and four children into a new $125,000 house with three acres of land, at 15500 Arapaho in Stanley, Kansas. The Robinson family was one of the first to move into the new Pleasant Valley Farms Estate in the upwardly-mobile Johnson County village. It was a smart, brand-new rural development, then way out in the country, with just one stop sign and no stores for miles.

His new neighbors knew nothing of his criminal past and regarded the slightly balding, thirty-three-year-old company president as very successful and definitely going places. Before long he was leading the Pleasant Valley Homeowners Association, although he had never officially been voted onto its board.

Over the next few years he re-invented himself as a pillar of the Stanley community, becoming a Scoutmaster, coaching the local tee-ball team, refereeing school volleyball games and buying two horses, so he could take an active role in several horse associations. He even took up religion again, becoming an elder at the Presbyterian Church of Stanley, where he taught Sunday school. The fact that he was Catholic did not seem to worry him in the least.

"He was quite a family man," remembered Jim Adams, who moved in next door to the Robinsons with his wife Mary in August 1978 and befriended the family. "He was a darned good father to his children and his eldest, John Jr., worshipped him."

Soon after arriving at Pleasant Valley, John Robinson formed a new company called Hydro-Gro Inc., and began looking for investors. The company sold water-based hydroponic kits, which allowed people to cultivate tomatoes, cucumbers and other vegetables inside their homes.

To launch the company, Robinson produced a glossy

color booklet entitled "If It Grows It Grows Better Hydroponically," which featured a photograph of his grinning five-year-old twins, Chris and Christy. A suitably immodest self-penned biography about the new Hydro-Gro president read: "We hope that as you read this book you will form an acquaintance with John Robinson as a sensitive and stimulating human being. John Robinson's lifetime goal in hydroponics is as far reaching as his imagination."

One of the first investors in the company was the recently retired Brooks Rickard, who was looking for a good investment to finance his wife Beth's medical bills for cancer. Brooks and his family put up $25,000 in Robinson's new venture and his daughter Nancy agreed to illustrate his gardening booklet.

During the preparation of the guide, Nancy Rickard found Robinson the perfect gentleman and "very encouraging," as he "coached" her through the work. But unfortunately the Rickards would lose every last cent they invested in Hydro-Gro.

In November 1977, Robinson devised an elaborate sting to further raise his own public profile by having himself appointed Kansas City's "Man of the Year." It was an award that did not exist until he invented it, with himself as the first beneficiary.

Eleven months earlier Robinson had done a minor consulting job for the Blue Valley Sheltered Workshop on Truman Road, Kansas City, and seen an opportunity for advancement. So when workshop president Robert G. O'Bryant resigned that spring, Robinson stood for the vacant post and got himself elected.

Former workshop director Paul Reiff said that Robinson had impressed everyone with his enthusiasm and appeared like a "young businessman; energetic, persuasive [and] likeable."

In early November, Robinson launched his campaign
to become man of the year by sending an official-looking
letter to then–Kansas City Mayor Charles B. Wheeler,
on behalf of the Kansas City Area Association of Sheltered Workshops. The letter invited the Mayor to a
planned luncheon in recognition of Kansas City businesses that had best assisted sheltered workshop programs.

"We would also like to invite you or a representative
from your office to be present for a small keynote
speech," read the letter, asking the Mayor to present the
Kansas City Area Association of Sheltered Workshops
Man of the Year Award.

Signed by J. E. Robinson, the letter included Hydro-
Gro's post office box address and telephone number in
case there were any questions.

Two weeks later, on November 17, the Mayor's office
received a follow-up letter purportedly signed by Paul
Reiff, as chairman of the Business Recognition Luncheon. It thanked the Mayor's secretary, Mildred Quinnett,
for the good news that Mayor Wheeler had approved "a
proclamation and commendation or a combination of the
two."

A few days later Robinson telephoned Quinnett, im-
personating Reiff, to make the final arrangements for the
luncheon. He said that both he and Robinson would be
at City Hall on December 5 at 10:00 a.m. to receive the
proclamation from the Mayor. That was two days prior
to the official luncheon, where State Senator Mary Gant
would present Robinson with his "Man of the Year"
plaque. Robinson had cunningly engineered Senator
Gant's appearance by asking Foundation Workshop marketing manager Harry Engle to find a dignitary to present
his award and make a speech in his honor. Engle then

asked his friend Senator Gant, who agreed to help out, believing it was a charity luncheon.

To ensure that his self-orchestrated award received suitable press coverage, Robinson prepared his own six-page typewritten press release, headlined: "Local Man Named Man of the Year," and sent it off to *The Kansas City Star*. It claimed that all information had been provided by his Sheltered Housing predecessor as president, Robert O'Bryant.

In an extensive profile he listed numerous purported achievements, claiming he was a registered X-ray technician, a medical laboratory technician and had been a consultant for more than 165 medical clinics and facilities. It also quoted tributes from many Kansas City medical professionals, who would all later deny making them. The press release was accompanied by a specially posed photograph of Robinson, looking every inch a captain of industry.

On December 7, fifty Kansas City businessmen, as well as Nancy Robinson and their children, attended the luncheon award ceremony. There was thunderous applause as John Robinson was presented with his award by Senator Gant, whose speech had even been written by Robinson, who had handed it to her in a manila envelope when she had arrived.

Paul Reiff still remembers Robinson's look of "fake surprise" as his award was announced and he stood up to accept it, feigning humility as he thanked the audience.

"I thought, This guy is bad news," Reiff would later say. "If he'll use an organization that's trying to help the disabled to his personal advantage, he'll stop at nothing."

The very next day the whole thing exploded in Robinson's face when *The Kansas City Star* printed a three-paragraph story about the award luncheon. The newspaper switchboard was soon flooded with protest calls complaining that it was a totally false story.

Somewhat embarrassed, the *Star* sent a reporter to investigate and, one week before his thirty-fourth birthday, the "Man of the Year" award was exposed as being a crooked John Robinson scheme. He was savaged in a hard-hitting story on page three, headlined "Man-of-the-Year Ploy Backfires on 'Honoree.' "

"A mayor, a state senator and a big city newspaper were unwitting puppets recently when a local businessman apparently decided to tinker with the news," it began. "The tinkerer was John E. Robinson Sr., a producer of kits used for growing plants without soil."

Reporter Mack Alexander raked Robinson over the coals, exposing his past criminal history and his run-in with the Securities and Exchange Commission. In an interview with *The Kansas City Star*, Robinson denied it all, saying he had "hoped the incident had been forgotten" and that he had only pleaded guilty because he "ran out of money to fight the charge."

He also denied using his position as president of the Blue Valley Sheltered Workshop to give himself the Man of the Year Award.

"We are left speechless, non-plussed," said Paul Reiff, the workshop's executive director, who had known nothing about the event of which he was supposed to be chairman. "You don't expect something like this to happen. You basically trust a person. When this sort of thing happens you don't know what to think."

A few weeks after the incident Robinson resigned his presidency of the Blue Valley Sheltered Workshop.

CHAPTER 4

HE'LL STOP AT NOTHING

ALTHOUGH the Man of the Year scandal was the talk of Kansas City, receiving extensive publicity in the press and on television, John Robinson's Hydro-Gro company survived. To build the business he began taking booths at local agricultural shows to promote his hydroponics kits and seek out new investors.

Margaret Adams first met Robinson at his stand at a trade show in 1978, where he was demonstrating his home-growing methods for tomatoes. At this time she did not realize that the suave-looking, dynamic businessman making her a sales pitch was her new Pleasant Valley neighbor.

"He and his staff were giving away tomatoes as a gimmick," she remembered. "I talked to him briefly and said I was interested in putting one of his units in my home."

Robinson was "as nice as can be" as he explained how his kits worked. But he soon moved on to the hard sell, telling Margaret his kits cost between three and four thousand dollars each. When she told him it was out of her price range, Robinson became "furious," accusing her of wasting his time.

"He was only interested in the big money," she said. "He was into investors and he said I was small time. He was really rough with me and very rude. He went hot and cold depending on whether you had anything for him."

A few weeks later, Margaret and her husband attended a meeting of the Pleasant Valley Homeowners

Association, where they met John and Nancy Robinson.

"Lo and behold, this man was our next-door neighbor," said Margaret. "I hadn't clicked."

After an uneasy introduction, Jim and Margaret Adams made up their differences with the Robinsons and both families started to socialize, their children becoming fast friends.

"Relations were very pleasant at first," said Margaret. "Christy used to come over and clip my strawberries, which she loved."

The Adamses' teenaged daughter Hilary, who was a classmate of John Robinson Jr. at Blue Valley High School, remembers Nancy as a "busy housewife," always cooking and cleaning the house, a cigarette constantly in her mouth.

"I thought it was weird that John Jr. always wore his scouting uniform to school even in his senior high school," said Hilary. "He played a musical instrument and was very involved in theater, but he didn't run in the same crowd that I did."

Initially, John Robinson Sr. did his best to create a good impression with his neighbors as the consummate family man. Some would even compare him to Ward Cleaver, the perfect dad of the 1960s hit television show, *Leave It to Beaver.*

Every Christmas he would dress up as Santa Claus and hand out presents at the annual Pleasant Valley children's party. Summer weekends would see him putting on his scout leader's uniform, to take his eldest son off to meetings. On several occasions he brought his scout pack home to go camping around the estate's communal pond.

But as residents got to know the Robinsons better, they began to realize it was all an elaborate charade and they were far from a happy family.

Hilary Adams remembers John Robinson Sr. as a "loud person" who often kept her awake at night, yelling at the kids. And another neighbor, Scott Davis, who became close friends with Robinson before falling victim to one of his scams some years later, remembers Nancy Robinson as a battered wife.

Scott's late parents, Bob and Dorothy Davis, would regularly socialize with the Robinsons over summer barbecues in their back yards, and were surrogate grandparents to their four children. Bob worked for a local nuclear medicine company and soon bonded with Robinson, who told him it was the same field he was in.

"Nancy was very good friends with my mother and she would confide in her," said Davis. "One day Nancy said John had beaten her up and slapped her around. But I would not necessarily call that S&M. It was more domestic battery."

One day Nancy called Scott into her house to ask him a favor. She wanted him to follow her husband, saying she suspected he was seeing another woman. Davis agreed but Robinson managed to lose him in downtown Kansas City before he could discover anything.

Soon after moving to Pleasant Valley, John Robinson built a stable on his land for the two horses he had bought his children, who already had a pet golden retriever called Casey. But before long neighbors were horrified at the way the animals were being treated. The horses looked scraggly and unnourished, as they were tethered for days outside the stable. Eventually someone called in the Humane Society to investigate.

"The horses were starving and so was the dog," said Mary Adams. "When I asked Nancy she said she didn't realize the food she was giving their golden retriever wasn't nutritional. Casey used to eat the cat food I put out for my pets, so I started feeding him because he looked so dreadful.

"The horses looked like they were ready for the glue factory. After the animal inspectors came around, Robinson was furious and soon got rid of them. He blamed me, although I never called the Humane Society. At the time we all said that anyone who starved their animals would do anything."

In March 1979 John Robinson jettisoned Hydro-Gro Inc. and found himself a day job as Employee Relations Manager at Guy's Foods, which manufactured potato chips and other fast-food snacks, in Liberty, Missouri. He had recently been discharged from federal probation with a glowing report from his probation officer, Ronald L. Ferguson. Yet again he seemed to have fooled the legal system.

"That you will continue to reap the rewards of good citizenship are the hopes of us all," Ferguson wrote in his official report.

It was a chaotic time at Guy's Foods, as it had just been sold to Borden Inc., so no one bothered to run a background check on the smartly-dressed executive, who'd failed to mention any criminal record in his written job application.

Situated about ten miles north of Kansas City on I-35, Liberty is a beautifully tranquil town, perhaps best known as the birthplace of outlaws Frank and Jesse James in the 1840s. It still retains a charming small-town atmosphere, attracting many people from Kansas City who want to escape the faster-paced pressures of urban living.

For a predator like John Robinson, Liberty was the perfect place to base his illegal operations.

Former Guy's operations manager, James Caldwell,

recalls Robinson as an outgoing, friendly type who fit in well with the other employees. But then large sums of money started to go missing.

Over the next nine months John Robinson looted Guy's for thousands of dollars in a variety of scams, much of the money never accounted for. And he started an affair with a secretary, who became his accomplice as she fell hopelessly in love with him.

Robinson even boasted to Scott Davis of inventing phantom Guy's employees, whose wages would then be paid directly into one of his own bank accounts. One day he gave Davis a demonstration of his expertise as a forger, using a Xerox copy machine and white-out to produce a convincing document with a fake signature on it.

"He'd love to brag about these things," said Davis. "You'd ask him, 'How are you going to get out of this one, John?' And he'd say, 'Here's where I'm good.' "

That August, Robinson took center stage at the annual Stanley Stampede town fair, when he arrived with an impressive fleet of miniature cars he'd gotten from a contact at Guy's Foods. Photographs show a grinning John Robinson dressed in full scouting uniform, racing the local children around a track in the tiny gasoline-driven vehicles.

Finally, Robinson's criminal activities at Guy's were exposed when the secretary gave him an ultimatum: leave Nancy and marry her or she'd go to the police. When he refused to walk out of his sixteen-year marriage, his secretary sold him down the river.

On December 30, 1980, John Robinson was fired from Guy's Foods and charged with Felony Theft six months later. Guy's Foods and Borden Inc. also filed a civil lawsuit, charging Robinson with submitting false vouchers and forged checks.

A subsequent internal investigation revealed that he had opened up a corporate bank account in Guy's Foods' name at the First National Bank of Liberty and used it to siphon off 8,662 dollars' worth of company checks for himself. He had also drawn nine checks totaling almost $20,000 directly on the Guy's Foods account, made payable to "fictitious persons and corporations" under his control. One for $3,900 was made out to his defunct Professional Services Association, Inc.

"It was the tip of the iceberg," said Caldwell, whose company sued Robinson for full restitution in the civil action.

Over the next few months Robinson and his lawyer, David Russell, kept the Clay County Court busy as he continued to maintain his innocence. Eventually he backed down with the overwhelming weight of evidence against him.

In the fall of 1981, the civil case was heard at Johnson County District Court and Robinson was ordered to pay $50,000 to Guy's Foods in restitution. Over the next four years he paid back more than $41,000, according to the Missouri Court of Appeals.

On December 3, 1981, John Robinson—a month short of his thirty-eighth birthday—pleaded guilty to a class C felony of stealing a $6,000 check from Guy's Foods, and cut a deal with the prosecutor. Although he faced a maximum sentence of seven years in jail, Robinson once again got off lightly, only having to serve sixty days of "shock time" at the Clay County Jail. He was also put on five years' probation under the Missouri Department of Probation and Parole.

"He was laughing before he went on the 'shock treatment,' as he referred to it," said Scott Davis. "He said it wasn't going to be a problem."

Soon after his arrest, Nancy filed for divorce after she

discovered the affair with his secretary. Her friends urged her to leave him for her own good, but after the couple went into counseling, she decided to remain in her miserable marriage for the sake of her four children.

"Nancy's friends and even her counselor advised her to leave him but she chose not to," said Davis. "My only theory is that her feeling of self-worth is so low, and she was so dependent on him, she just couldn't break it."

At 1:30 p.m on May 8, 1982, John Robinson arrived at the Clay County Court to start his sentence. He and Nancy told their children he was going away on a business trip and somehow the case never made *The Kansas City Star*. But word did get out in Stanley and the Robinson children found themselves in a difficult position at Blue Valley High School.

"I remember the embarrassed looks on his kids' faces when I passed them in the hall in high school," said Hilary Adams.

When he left jail in July, Robinson seemed proud to have served time, even boasting to Scott Davis how he had received "special treatment" from the warden, who now wanted to become his partner in a bar in Liberty.

"There was no shame. There was no remorse. It was more like a joke," remembers Davis.

That summer John Robinson started a new consulting company called Equi-Plus. When asked the origin of the name he would explain that he named his company for equity, plus anything else he could get.

Hiring a small staff and installing Nancy as secretary, Robinson rented a plush office suite at 10550 Barkley in the upscale Kansas City suburb of Overland Park, and erected a large "Equi-Plus" sign outside. He also printed a full-color brochure to attract investors for the marketing company, which was seeking new products to develop and bring to market.

Among the unlikely collection of early projects Equi-Plus put into development was a technique for storing bull sperm to impregnate cows and a bar basketball game, which Robinson hoped would capture the growing leisure market. Two of its first clients were Scott Davis and his father Bob, who were well aware of Robinson's criminal history. And it was they who would introduce Robinson to computers for the first time.

The Davises had launched a company called Online Computers in August 1981 but soon ran into financial problems. When Robinson heard of their plight, he immediately offered the services of Equi-Plus to find venture capital and get Online Computers into the black.

"He was invited to try and figure out what was wrong and help manage it," explained Scott Davis. "We signed a contract to pay Equi-Plus thirty percent if he obtained investors or if it was sold. That was a fair rate."

Robinson and his staff went into action, holding weekly business meetings with the Davises and advising them on streamlining the company for maximum efficiency. A few weeks later he told Scott he had organized a $300,000 line of bank credit to bail out the sinking computer company. A meeting was arranged between the bank and Davis, with Robinson and his current attorney present.

But when Davis and Robinson met in his attorney's office, in one of the seedier parts of Kansas City, Davis sensed the loan might be mob-related.

"It was a very nondescript building from the outside," remembers Davis. "I walked in and we were told to wait in the lobby by the attorney's secretary for a long time. I had noticed that the door was ajar so I peeked through. Inside was sort of like a tavern, which hadn't been cleaned up from the night before. But what amazed me was a picture of Mussolini with an Italian flag, hanging over the bar. Then the secretary came back and when she saw me looking in, she quickly closed the door and told me to wait outside."

Finally his attorney appeared and the three men drove to the bank to meet the president and discuss the loan. During the ride it was agreed that Robinson and his lawyer would each receive $30,000 commission, if the refinancing loan was approved.

At the brief ten-minute meeting Davis became even more suspicious that something shady was going on. The bank president only asked him a couple of basic questions about his computer business, before telling him to leave with Robinson so he could finalize the loan with the attorney.

"That was bullshit," said Davis. "They just said they would take care of it."

Two weeks went by and there was still no news on the loan. So Davis called up the bank to discover it had been shut down by the Feds and was presently under investigation.

In 1983 Online Computers finally went out of business and filed Chapter Eleven. John Robinson was furious when he realized there would be no money to pay him for his services. When his attorney demanded Robinson be placed at the top of the creditors' list, he was told to get in line like everyone else.

Then Robinson produced a contract, purported to have been signed by Bob Davis, saying he would be paid $30,000 no matter what happened to the company.

"It was forged," said Scott Davis, who well-remembered the demonstration Robinson had staged for him a couple of years earlier. "I told him if he wanted to pursue this I'd take him to court."

Robinson then sent an intimidating letter to Davis' mother Dorothy, who was still best friends with his wife Nancy. It stated that he was organizing the creditors to fight, warning her that she would lose her home and be out on the street if he didn't get his money.

"Those were the depths he sunk to," said Davis. "My mother, who was an invalid, was very upset and hurt by this. As far as I was concerned he was a cold, plain unethical bastard."

The Davises refused to pay him a cent and Robinson eventually gave up trying to get the money and moved on.

John Robinson was also making his presence felt in Pleasant Valley, where once again he was the subject of much gossip. Word was that he had sexually propositioned some of his neighbors' wives, and on at least one occasion a jealous husband had confronted Robinson and blows were exchanged.

Another time a neighbor's dog ran into the path of John Jr.'s bicycle, causing him to take a bad fall. His volatile father flew into a fury, charging over to the dog owner's house and threatening to beat him up.

All the bad feeling and hostility at Pleasant Valley proved highly embarrassing for Nancy Robinson and her four children.

"Nancy went around like she was trying to fold in on herself and disappear," said Margaret Adams. "She looked like she had early osteoporosis and she was only in her thirties. I don't know if it actually was or if she was just plain browbeaten."

John Robinson's abrasive attitude and obsessive need to control was like poison, slowly infecting Pleasant Valley, and proved highly divisive. At one point he tried to take over the Homeowners Association and run the estate. He became very unpopular when he passed a motion forcing everyone to clean up their part of the bridle path surrounding the estate. It was noted that Robinson only had about thirty feet of path to maintain, while everyone else had at least six hundred feet of trees to cut and grass to mow.

The neighbors were also puzzled when he constructed an elaborate fish pond at the edge of his property, even though there was already one on the estate.

But things came to a head after a female resident's house burned to the ground, after being struck by lightning. When it was re-built with a fire-resistant composite-shingle roof, instead of the Homeowners' approved wooden one, John Robinson personally took the owner to court, saying it was lowering the value of his house.

"He pitted neighbor against neighbor and we've all been rather distant even to this day," remembers Jim Adams, whose wife Margaret went to court on behalf of the owner.

The matter was eventually settled by placing a wooden roof over the composite one to pacify John Robinson.

In early 1982 John Robinson recruited a partner in crime, named Irv Blattner, who was also on probation. A freelance sound and video technician, Blattner worked on several projects for Equi-Plus and found himself increasingly drawn into Robinson's illegal activities.

Recently, Robinson's bold claims to prospective clients and investors had become more and more outlandish. He boasted of being a Hollywood movie mogul, single-handedly raising capital for Sylvester Stallone's recent blockbuster *First Blood*. He also bragged of his "extensive experience" raising venture capital for cattle breeding operations and oil and gas exploration ventures. Unfortunately for his gullible investors, none of these claims were true.

In December, one of Robinson's partners, Ted Findlay, who had invested $10,000 in Equi-Plus, lost every cent. Six months later when he complained, Robinson told him their company was "defunct."

Although he had had little success as a white-collar criminal, the ever-confident Robinson now enlarged his Equi-Plus empire to start a sister company called Equi-II. On the surface Equi-II was a management consultant firm that would involve itself in a wide range of commercial ventures.

And over the next two years Robinson would allegedly enlarge his criminal operations to include murder, prostitution and baby-selling.

CHAPTER 5

THE VANISHING

In May 1984 Irv Blattner brought John Robinson to 4518 Campbell in Kansas City, Missouri, to meet Mildred Amadi, a former tenant of his who wanted a divorce. Posing as an attorney, Robinson carefully listened to how she had married a Nigerian man in a marriage of convenience so he could remain in the U.S. He then offered to get her an immediate divorce, in return for $200 in cash and her 1976 American Motors car. Amadi agreed to his terms, handing him the title to her car as well as her birth and marriage certificates. There and then Robinson drew up an agreement, which she signed.

Two months later John Robinson repaid Blattner by helping him to get an administrative job with one of his Equi-II clients, the Midwest College of Medical Associates in Kansas City.

By mid-January 1985, Mildred Amadi still didn't know whether she was married or not. In desperation she complained to Johnson County Assistant District Attorney Steve Obermeier, claiming that the "bum" had told her she was officially divorced and to get on with her life.

"I [still] don't know if I'm divorced," said the distressed woman, after a futile attempt to find her divorce certificate in the courthouse in Olathe. "He keeps telling me I'm divorced, go out, get married. [But] I don't want to go to jail."

Soon afterwards Robinson summoned her to an Overland Park hotel where he assured her the divorce was going through, giving her two hundred dollars that he claimed was from her husband. Later when asked to explain himself to his probation officer, Steve Haymes, Robinson denied everything, claiming Amadi had made it all up and had merely asked him to find her husband.

No legal action was ever taken against Robinson after Amadi's complaint. Now, it seems, he believed he could get away with anything—maybe even murder.

In the summer of 1984 John Robinson placed an advertisement in a local paper for a new sales representative for Equi-II. One of the applicants was a shy, nineteen-year-old girl named Paula Godfrey, who had graduated from Olathe North High School the previous year and sought a career in business.

Born on June 19, 1965, Paula was the eldest of three children of Olathe businessman Bill Godfrey. She was a natural athlete and began ice-skating at the age of five, passionately devoting herself to the sport with hopes of one day turning professional. The dark-haired girl was such a dedicated figure skater that she regularly got up at 4:00 a.m. for morning practice at the King Louie Ice Chateau on Metcalf, and would return again after school.

A vivacious, pretty girl, Paula was on the honor roll for her junior and senior years at Olathe North and her yearbook shows she was an active member of an unofficial cheerleaders' club called the Senior Rowdies. Her chemistry teacher Greg Kifer remembers Paula as "a good kid" with a "good sense of humor."

After graduating with good grades in summer 1983, her life-long dreams of turning professional were dashed when she tried out for a coveted place in the Walt Disney World On Ice Show during a bout of flu and didn't perform well. Bill Godfrey says his slim, five-foot-eight-inch daughter had planned to try again the following year, but in the meantime she responded to John Robinson's Equi-II advertisement.

"I didn't know anything about it," said her father, who at the time was out of town on business. "She discussed it with my wife and went for an interview and then I guess the supposed job."

Paula got the job and came home after her interview with Robinson, telling her mother how nice her new boss was and how the job would give her an excellent start in business. She said Robinson had also promised to fly her, and several other new female employees, to San Antonio, Texas, for a special course in clerical skills.

On September 1, 1984, John Robinson arrived at the Godfreys' house and collected Paula to drive her to Kansas City International Airport for her flight to San Antonio.

"And that's the last time we saw her," said her emotional father fifteen years later.

The first night Paula—who was extremely close to her parents, and brother Brad and sister Shannon—failed to call and her family became concerned when she didn't contact them the following day. When Bill Godfrey still hadn't heard a word from her four days later, he was so worried he flew out to San Antonio to try to find her and discovered that Paula had never even checked into the hotel where she was supposedly staying.

On his return to Olathe he filed a missing persons report and hired a private detective. Then he drove to Equi-II's offices to confront John Robinson.

"He acted very surprised," said Godfrey. "I told him that I better hear from my daughter in three days."

A couple of days later a short, handwritten note bearing a Kansas City postmark and supposedly written by Paula, arrived at the Godfrey home. Although it assured her parents she was fine, Godfrey thought it "very out-of-character" and took it straight to the police.

Soon afterwards the Overland Park Police Department received another handwritten letter that they assumed was from Paula, saying she was OK and thankful for all John Robinson's help. She said she was now living in western Kansas and did not want to see her family.

"Oh, I knew he did it," said Godfrey. "I don't think it was her handwriting. We weren't mad at her and she wasn't mad at us. She was a mature young lady looking to be involved in business."

Incredibly, after receiving the letter the Overland Police Department called off its missing persons investigation, satisfied there was no evidence of any wrongdoing.

"After the first six months we felt like she was dead," said Godfrey, "and we had two other children we had to be concerned about, so we had to move on. We did all we could at the time but there didn't seem to be many answers from the police."

Years later another letter from Paula would surface, this time addressed to John Robinson. The badly-typed letter, full of profanities and grammatical mistakes, appears to have been designed for the benefit of someone named Ralph. It explains the theft of some money and a car, laying the blame on the innocent, well-educated teenager, who had never been known to use bad language.

John:

I am really sorry about this but you have just been fucked out of your money! I also took your car, I will write and let either you or that dumb shit Ralph know were [sic] I leave the car. I would imagine that Larry is really going to be pissed at you, I—ot [sic] you

[sic] money, your car, Ralphs [sic] money and Larrys [sic] shit. Not a bad haul in one day.

Tell Ralphie that it serves him right for treating me sooooooo bad! I gave him everything and got nothing back in return from him. I don't know what he wants. His kid was over the other day at his place and he doesn't even want to stay.

I hope you understand. I didn't want to screw you up and I know Larry is going to be looking for me, but by the time you read this I will be long gone. If you go to the cops about your car, I will have to tell them all about your dealings and Raphs [sic] too. So jsut [sic] both of you be cool. I will make sure you know how to get your car back. I haven't decided on cleveland [sic], chicago or denver, oh well.

Love ya,
Paula

Shortly after the letter was written, Irv Blattner stumbled across it in Robinson's office. By this time he had fallen out with Robinson and was cooperating with the Secret Service, who were trying to build a case against his former friend for illegally cashing a government check. Fearing Robinson might try to harm him, he photocopied the letter and placed it with another one, in which Robinson accused him of betrayal. Then he put them both in an Equi-II envelope and hid them at his house as future insurance.

A frightened Blattner told friends he now feared for his life and believed Paula Godfrey may have been murdered by Robinson. If anything were ever to happen to him they should give the letters to the FBI.

When Blattner died from cancer in the early nineties a relative sorting through his things found the letters still hidden in the bottom of a briefcase. It would be a smoking gun, leading straight to Robinson fifteen years after Paula Godfrey's mysterious disappearance.

Just prior to having placed the recruitment ad in the paper, John Robinson took out a lease in the name of Equi-II on a duplex at 8110 Troost Avenue, the low-rent dividing line between white and black neighborhoods in Kansas City, Missouri. According to investigators at the time, he had decided to start a new career as a pimp, recruiting an experienced prostitute named Linda Stevens-Jones (not her real name) and instructed her to run the brothel. Then he began finding girls to move into the duplex and service his customers.

Advertising by word of mouth and in underground sex magazines, Robinson allegedly soon owned a highly lucrative operation. It reportedly specialized in rough, sado-masochistic sex, something John Robinson had secretly enjoyed for years. Now he began spending more and more time satisfying his kinky lust for torture and domination. And he began to search out willing sex slaves for the use of his contacts in the twilight world of BDSM.

Over the last few years, he had also apparently become a leading member of a bizarre, highly secret S&M cult called the International Council of Masters. Years later Robinson would have one of his slaves post its amazing history on the Internet to recruit new members.

The council had its beginnings on November 12, 1920, in the backroom of a London, England, pub. That fateful night six professional men, including leaders of the legal, medical and financial professions, decided to start a club to cater to their unusual sexual tastes, in the tradition of the infamous Marquis de Sade.

"Each knew the other to be a forthright person and one who could be counted on to maintain a strict code of silence," according to the Internet posting. "On that evening each in turn discussed their personal situation and revealed that they were Dominant men who maintained submissive females as their personal servants."

The six men agreed to form an association to be known as the Masters Guild, with a restrictive membership by invitation only. They agreed to be bound by a code of silence and drafted a strict set of rules and rituals for meetings, including that each member must buy and maintain three pieces of equipment for a communal dungeon.

The first meeting of the Masters Guild was held in the basement of a London warehouse at 8:00 p.m. on Friday, May 13, 1921.

"The date of the meeting was chosen because these men thought of themselves as a cult," the Internet history continued. "They knew that if their personal perversion became known to the public they would be ruined."

The chronicle then described the historic first meeting which set the seal of rituals still practiced by the cult to this day:

> The first meeting began with now seven men entering the room clothed only in a purple hooded robe. After a few moments, each man in turn left the room and returned with his bound slave. Each slave wore metal cuffs connected to chains and a simple white robe tied at the waist with a purple cord.

> Then, after all the slaves were assembled, each assuming a kneeling, submissive position, the slaves were instructed, one by one, to rise. When they did, each Master untied his slave's robe and let it fall to the ground, revealing her body to the entire group. Following this "initial instruction" of slaves came the "training," as

each Master chose his particular piece of equipment.

Over the next several years, meetings were held on a monthly basis and as the Guild grew, more and more rules and formalities were developed. A committee was even established to supervise formal trading of female slaves between members and settle any disputes.

Within five years the Guild had proved so popular that a second branch was started. And eventually the Masters Guild would spread its dark tentacles all over Europe until it finally reached America, where it now has dungeons from coast to coast.

On August 13, 1982 its name was officially changed to the International Council of Masters, to reflect its new global status.

Kansas City investigative journalist Kevin Petrehm of the NBC affiliate KSHB-TV, has carried out extensive research on the cult. He discovered that John Robinson held a key position when he interviewed a former female member, who had spent many years active in it before leaving.

"Robinson was the cult's Slavemaster and it was a position he excelled at," explained Petrehm. "His job was to bring a victim to meetings for either beatings, torture or rape."

The former member—who claims to have been sexually mutilated as a punishment for trying to leave—picked out Robinson from a photograph, saying he was very near the top of the cult's chain of command. She also told Petrehm about at least three young girls, always heavily drugged, whom Robinson led into meetings on a collared chain leash.

"She didn't believe they even knew what was going on," said Petrehm. "One of them did try and get away from Robinson once but was restrained."

CHAPTER 6

LISA AND TIFFANY

ON December 18, 1984, Missouri Probation Officer Steve Haymes received an alarming telephone call, revealing a frightening new dimension to John Robinson's criminal activities. Ann Smith from Birthright, a local charity that helps young pregnant mothers before and after the delivery of their babies, told Haymes that she had been contacted by Robinson and was highly suspicious.

A few days earlier he'd telephoned, claiming that he represented the First Presbyterian Church of Stanley, which was developing a six-month program to help young women who had just given birth. The church, he said, would be prepared to board a young mother, who fit his criteria, in an Olathe duplex for $125 a month and pay her $800 a month plus expenses, until she and her baby got back on their feet.

"Robinson wanted to know if Birthright had any young women who might fit that profile," wrote the young probation officer in his report.

The day before Smith called Haymes, a Birthright worker named Barbara Bergman had brought a young girl, who had just had a baby, to an Olathe restaurant for an interview with Robinson. Over lunch he told them about his three years working for the church's outreach, saying the program had a duplex in Olathe that accommodated six girls. When Bergman asked him the name of the program, he seemed to stumble, saying it was called "Trans Tech," and he could not remember the director's name or its phone number.

Robinson then asked the young mother what she wanted to do in life. She told him she was interested in silk-screening, and he mentioned a school he knew in Dallas that might be suitable, although again he couldn't remember exact specifics.

"He pressed that he wanted the girl in the program by Christmas," Haymes wrote. When Bergman asked him exactly where the duplex was located in Olathe, Robinson hedged, saying he wasn't exactly sure.

Bergman then sent the young mother outside to wait in her car and confided that she had a history of drug problems and her mother was in a mental institution. Robinson then visibly lost interest, saying he had to leave for an appointment.

After the meeting Bergman began to suspect Robinson's motives and decided to investigate. She called the First Presbyterian Church of Stanley and was told that although they knew of John Robinson, he was not officially affiliated with them and there was no such program to help unfortunate young mothers. She then checked with an Olathe bank where Robinson claimed to be on the board of directors. They too had never heard of him.

When Bergman told Ann Smith of her suspicions, she did her own checking, leading her straight to Robinson's probation officer, Steve Haymes, at the Missouri Division of Probation and Parole.

After Smith's phone call Haymes contacted Judge John R. Hutcherson to apprise him of the strange situation. The judge agreed that Robinson was acting suspiciously, saying it may be necessary to hold a court hearing and add new probation conditions to stop his fraudulent misrepresentations. He also told Haymes to investigate further, placing the full resources of the probation service at his disposal.

Soon afterwards Haymes called Robinson's Olathe probation officer, Christina Thornbrugh, who said she had no "difficulties" with Robinson and was stunned to learn that he might be involved in prostitution and selling babies. Haymes promised to keep her informed of any further developments.

It would be another fifteen years before Steve Haymes discovered the true reason that Robinson had wanted a young mother and baby in time for Christmas—back in Chicago Robinson's younger brother Donald and his wife Helen were having problems having a baby of their own. At a Robinson family reunion in Stanley, Kansas, in the summer of 1983, Donald, who managed a Chicago Radio Shack, had asked his brother for advice about private adoption, explaining that the local Catholic charity adoption fees were "exorbitant."

Robinson had immediately seen an opportunity, saying he knew an attorney who specialized in adoptions and would talk to him. In May 1984 John called his brother with some exciting news. He had found them a child for adoption and asked them to send a check for $2,500 made out to Equi-II, promising they would have their baby by October. He assured them it would all be perfectly legal and he would supply the necessary paperwork.

Donald and Helen Robinson spent the next few months joyfully planning for their new arrival. They set up a nursery in their Chicago home and bought baby clothes, toys and diapers, and even ordered a crib on layaway.

But October came and went without any sign of a baby, with Robinson explaining that there had been problems with the adoption and they would just have to wait. In the weeks leading up to Christmas, he was actively searching for a newborn baby to present his family, who had agreed to pay him another $3,000 as the final adoption fee.

A week before Christmas, after striking out with Birthright, Robinson called the Truman Medical Center in Kansas City, and set up a meeting with Karen Gaddis and Sharon Jackson Turner, who were social workers for the hospital's obstetrics department. He claimed to represent a consortium of fifteen successful Overland Park businessmen who wanted to give something back to the community and had set up the Kansas City Outreach Program to help girls with young babies.

The smooth-talking Robinson impressed the two social workers with his detailed knowledge of local Catholic charities and social service groups. He also reeled off a list of his contacts in big business, claiming to have already approached IBM and Xerox for donations to the program.

"The guy presented himself as if he was the president of the Jaycees," Gaddis would later remember. "He knew everything he needed to know. He knew names, he knew agencies . . . he had an answer for everything."

Gaddis would later admit she was slightly skeptical when Robinson stressed the importance of there being a 50–50 racial mix with the mothers. But when they questioned it he explained that this had been stipulated by the "contributors," and urged them to find a white girl for his program.

Said Gaddis: "He'd say, 'You know, I don't really care about this, but can you tell me is the mother white or black?' "

There was also a slight problem when Robinson told them his duplex was in Olathe, as it was out of their hospital catchment area and not in their area of need. But a couple of days later Robinson called back with the good news that he had secured an apartment at 8110

Troost Avenue, which had been donated by a local businessman. There would also be a second one available in the same building within a month.

Robinson stressed it was imperative that a young mother and baby move in by the Saturday after Christmas, as Xerox or IBM were sending someone from New York to inspect the program.

A few days later the social workers found a black girl at the Truman Medical Center whom they thought would be suitable. But Robinson turned her down, repeating that the program had to have a white mother and baby.

As there were no other young mothers available at the publicly-funded hospital, where most patients were black, Gaddis and Turner checked with other agencies. Finally, according to the case notes of Robinson's probation officer, they came up with a Caucasian mother who had a four-month-old baby and was presently staying at the Hope House Battered Women's Center.

Although he hadn't quite made his Christmas deadline to find his brother a baby, he would only be a few days late.

Lisa Stasi was a beautiful nineteen-year-old girl with a radiant smile that belied the hardships of her short life. Born Lisa Ellidge in Huntsville, Alabama, on April 11 1965, her father had died when she was a child, and one of her brothers had committed suicide. She and her other brother Marty were brought up by her mother but throughout her teenage years she struggled for a sense of identity, leaving high school with few qualifications.

In 1983, at the age of seventeen, she moved to Kansas City to start a new life. She knew no one and spent the first few months there drifting. One night she walked into the Stein Bar in the Italian quarter of Kansas City, where she struck up a conversation with the barmaid, Kathy Rogers.

Although the pretty, slim girl with sad blue eyes and newly-dyed red hair was clearly underage, Kathy served her a beer and they struck up a conversation. After hearing that she had nowhere to go, Kathy invited Lisa to stay at her house until she found somewhere permanent.

"I felt sorry for her because she was only a couple of years younger than my son," remembers Kathy. "She was a lost soul and just a very lonely person."

Over the next two months Kathy became a surrogate mother and friend to Lisa, listening to her problems and giving her advice. But Lisa would never discuss her troubled past or her family back in Huntsville.

Lisa was soon accepted into the lively crowd of Stein Bar regulars, spending most nights there, partying. And before long she had fallen in love with Carl Stasi, a young sailor who also frequented the bar.

"She was very much attached to Carl," says Rogers, who watched their relationship blossom. "All Lisa wanted in life was to love and be loved and to have a happy normal life."

In August 1984, Lisa, eight months pregnant, married Carl in a small civic ceremony in Huntsville, Alabama, with her family present. A month later, on September 3, Lisa gave birth to a baby girl at Truman Medical Center in Kansas City, Missouri. The couple named her Tiffany Lynn.

But Lisa's happiness was short-lived. The marriage reportedly turned violent and collapsed acrimoniously a month after Tiffany's birth. Seeking protection, Lisa and her new baby then moved into Hope House, a shelter for battered women in Kansas City.

At the beginning of January, Lisa was called into the office of Hope House social worker Cathy Stackpole, to hear some good news. A local philanthropist had heard about her and Tiffany's plight and wanted to help. He had offered her a place in his new Kansas City Outreach program as well as training for a new career.

Lisa was delighted when Stackpole told her she and Tiffany could immediately move into the program's apartment for nothing. Then she would go to Dallas, Texas, to train to become a silk-screen printer and even receive a generous $800-a-month stipend, as well as extra money for baby-sitting. Later, she was told, there would be further job opportunities in Chicago, Denver or Kansas City.

"She was real excited and thought she was going to start a new life for her and her daughter," said Lisa's aunt, Karen Moore.

A couple of days later Lisa and Tiffany left Hope House and went to her sister-in-law Kathy Klinginsmith's house, where her benefactor had arranged to collect them. While they were waiting, Lisa excitedly told Kathy and her husband David about the Kansas Outreach Program and how it would help her get a job and a high-school equivalency degree.

"I kind of quizzed her because I was pretty concerned about the situation," Kathy would later remember. "It just didn't sound right."

John Robinson arrived at the Klinginsmiths' home in Northeast Kansas City in the midst of a heavy snowstorm, wearing a long brown trench coat. Kathy and David helped Lisa and her baby to his car and kissed them goodbye. Lisa promised to return soon and collect her own Toyota Corolla, which still had Tiffany's toys, baby food and diapers in the trunk. Then Robinson drove them away into the raging blizzard.

* * *

Lisa Stasi would never know her alleged killer's real name. When John Robinson checked her and Tiffany into Room 131 at the Overland Park Rodeway Inn on Tuesday, January 8, 1985, he used the name "Mr. John Osborne," paying with an Equi-II company credit card. The motel was at the junction of I-435 and Metcalf, just a few blocks away from the Equi-II offices.

Over the next two days John Robinson apparently talked to Lisa about her life, cunningly discovering pertinent details about her friends and family that he would use later. She mentioned a traffic accident she'd recently been involved in and how her car was about to be repossessed, as she couldn't afford the payments. She also told him about her short, unhappy marriage and how her brother Marty was pressuring her and Tiffany to move to Alabama and care for a needy aunt.

On Wednesday evening, the night after Robinson had brought her to the Rodeway Inn, a sobbing Lisa called her mother-in-law, Betty Stasi. She demanded to know why Carl—who did not know his wife and daughter had left Hope House, as he was away on a naval assignment—was divorcing her. She also accused Betty of trying to get custody of Tiffany, saying she'd seen signed affidavits to this effect. She also cryptically remarked that she had just signed four blank sheets of paper which she had given to "them."

At one point in the heated conversation Lisa became hysterical, shouting: "Here they are! Can't talk!" Then she hung up the phone.

Early Thursday morning, January 10, there was a heavy snow falling as Lisa and Tiffany checked out of the Rodeway Inn and disappeared forever. It would be another fifteen years before Tiffany would resurface—as John Robinson's adopted niece.

* * *

The following morning Donald and Helen Robinson flew into Kansas City International Airport, where they were met by a beaming John Robinson. He appeared delighted to have finally found them a baby to adopt, telling them that her mother had tragically committed suicide in a hotel room a few days earlier.

He then drove them straight to his Equi-II office to sign what he claimed were adoption papers. To seal the adoption Donald gave his brother a $3,000 cashier's check made out to his attorney on top of the $2,500 check he had previously given him in May.

Then Robinson took them to his home where they were welcomed at the front door by Nancy, who was holding little Tiffany Stasi, wearing a beautiful new dress. Donald and Helen were overjoyed to meet their new daughter for the first time, and told John and Nancy they planned to call her Heather Tiffany.

"We had originally planned on naming her Heather Elise," Donald Robinson would later testify. "But we changed to Heather Tiffany because that was the name that her mother wanted her to have."

The next day Robinson drove Donald and Helen back to the airport, where they flew home to Chicago with their beautiful new baby girl to start their new life together. Before they left John had organized a group family photograph, with Nancy, their four children and Donald and Helen. And right in the center was a smiling John Robinson proudly holding his new niece, Heather Tiffany, high above a little rocking horse.

On Saturday, January 12, Kathy Klinginsmith called the Overland Park Police Department to report Lisa and Tiffany missing. She told them about the mysterious Mr. Osborne whom she had briefly seen when he collected them a couple of days earlier. That afternoon her husband, David, stormed into Equi-II's offices at Metcalf Avenue and 98th Street to demand an explanation and find out what had happened to Lisa and Tiffany.

David Klinginsmith would later tell Overland Park police that, while there, he spoke to an unknown man, who became very upset and pushed him out of the office. A few hours later Klinginsmith received a mysterious telephone call from someone claiming to be "Father Martin," a priest from the City Union Mission. He left a message that Lisa and Tiffany were fine and gave his phone number. But when Klinginsmith tried the number it was residential and no one knew of any Father Martin. He also checked with City Union Mission who informed him they had no priests working there.

The following day Cathy Stackpole of Hope House received a typed letter. It was signed by Lisa Ellidge Stasi and dated January 10, the day of her disappearance.

Dear Cathy:

I want to thank you for all your help. I have decided to get away from this area and try and make a good life for me and Tiffany. Marty my brother want [sic] me to go take care of my aunt but I don't want to. He is trying to take over my life and I just am not going to let him. I borrowed some money from a friend and Tiffany and I are leaving Kansas City. The people you referred me to were really nice and helped me with everything. I am very greatful [sic] for everyones [sic] help.

I wrote to the outreach people, Carl's mother and my brother telling them all that I had made the decision to get a fresh start in life. If I stay here they will just try and run my life more and more like they are trying to do. I finally realized that I have a baby to take care of and she is my first responsibility. I asked my brother to tell the bank to pick up the car because the tags have expired and I am so far behind with the payments that I could never get them up to date, and with no job the bank wants the car or the money. I will be fine, I know what I want and I am going to go after it. Again thanks for your help and Hope House and thanks for telling me about outreach. Everyone has been so helpful I owe you all a great deal.

The next day Betty Stasi also received a letter bearing Lisa's signature, written just hours after David Klinginsmith had visited Equi-II. But instead of pacifying the Stasi family, it only made them more concerned for Lisa and Tiffany's safety.

Betty knew that Lisa could not type and the letter did not sound like her at all. She also clearly remembered her daughter-in-law saying that "they" had made her sign four blank sheets of paper.

Betty

Thank you for all your help I really do appreciate it! I have decided to leave Kansas City and try and make a new life for myself and Tiffany. I wrote to Marty and told him to let the bank take the car back, the payments are so far behind that they either want the money or the car. I don't have the money to pay the bank all the back payments and the car needs a lot of work. When I wrote Marty about the car I forgot to tell him that I left the lock box with all my papers in the trunk. Since the accident I couldn't get the trunk opened. Please tell him to force open the trunk and get that box of papers out before the bank gets the car.

Thanks for all your help, but I really need to get

away and start a new life for me and Tiffany. She
deserves a real mother who works and takes care of
her. The people at Hope House and Outreach were
really helpful, but I just couldn't keep taking charity
from them. I feel that I have to get out on my own
and prove that I can handle it myself.

Marty wanted me to go to Alabama to take care
of aunt Evelyn but I just can't. She is so opinionated
and hard to get along with right now I just can't deal
with her. Marty and I fought about it and I know he
will try and force me to go to Alabama. I am just not
going there.

I will let you know from time to time how I am
and what I am doing. Tell Carl that I will write him
and let him know where he can get in touch with me.

A few days later, according to Steve Haymes' case
notes, John Robinson phoned Karen Gaddis, asking if
she had heard from Lisa. He said she and Tiffany had
disappeared from the Rodeway Inn, leaving all their belongings in the room. Sometime later he called back,
saying that he had found them and they were safe. But
then he called a third time, claiming Lisa had disappeared once again, leaving a note for him at the Troost
Avenue apartment. According to Robinson, Lisa had
written that she had met a man named Bill and they'd
gone off together to Denver, Colorado.

He then told Gaddis that he couldn't believe her in-
gratitude, after all the trouble he had gone to to help her
and her baby.

CHAPTER 7

AN INVESTIGATION

STEVE Haymes began investigating John Robinson at the beginning of January 1985, but would always be one step behind. As Robinson was checking Lisa and Tiffany Stasi into the Overland Park Rodeway Inn, Haymes was interviewing Birthright's Barbara Bergman, who told him about her strange meeting with Robinson three weeks earlier.

Ironically, on the very day the Stasis went missing, Haymes sent Robinson a letter, asking him to come to his office the following week. When he received no reply, Haymes sent a registered letter to get Robinson's attention. On January 21, an apologetic Robinson telephoned to explain that he had been in Denver, Colorado, on business and had not seen the letter. He agreed to meet Haymes in his office three days later.

Toward the end of the conversation, Robinson casually asked if there was "a problem." Haymes told him that he preferred to "talk to him face to face" about "this incident."

A few hours before the scheduled meeting, Steve Haymes contacted FBI Special Agent Ed Humphrey to see if Robinson was under investigation and if they knew of any "baby-selling rings," using a similar charity scenario to find victims. Agent Humphrey checked and then called back, saying that the FBI knew of Robinson but he was not presently under investigation. The agency was also not aware of any baby-selling currently in the Kansas City area.

At exactly 1:00 p.m. a confident John Robinson arrived at the Missouri Probation Office and walked into Haymes' office, where his case file was laid out on the desk. Haymes came straight to the point, asking for an explanation of his dealings with Birthright.

Robinson freely admitted calling the organization in connection with a "charitable situation" he was involved in. He then told his probation officer that he and five Kansas City business associates had been sitting around talking one day and decided on a plan to return something to the community, as a thank-you for their success. When Haymes asked their names Robinson refused to answer, suggesting he talk to his attorney, Ron Wood, who was aware of Kansas City Outreach.

Robinson also claimed to have held discussions with "numerous" other Kansas City social agencies, as well as a priest. He said they had all expressed great interest in his program.

Haymes then steered his questions to 8110 Troost Avenue, the Kansas City apartment he suspected Robinson of using as a brothel. His probationer said he had rented it through his Equi-II company, adding that he had already helped several young women with small children.

"Robinson stated that at the present time, Kansas City Outreach had two young women living [there]," Haymes wrote at the time, noting that Robinson had invited him to come and inspect the premises.

Robinson then explained how the Kansas City Outreach program worked, saying all the prospective applicants must be referrals from a social agency. The mothers had to be at least twenty-one years old and have had their babies less than six months. If they met the program's requirements, the mothers and babies would receive emergency housing for a maximum of three months.

Asked what his own personal liability was if anything

was to go wrong while they were in his care, Robinson didn't miss a beat. He explained that under the rules all the girls had to sign a liability waiver when they first entered the program, to absolve him from all legal responsibility. They were also given a set of regulations to read, as well as an overview of Kansas City Outreach. Finally they were asked to fill out a detailed questionnaire about their own personal details.

Then, fixing Robinson straight in the eye, Haymes asked what he was getting out of all this philanthropy. Robinson looked hurt, replying that he was "getting the satisfaction of being a help to the community and people less fortunate than himself." His attorney would soon be filing papers to register it as a charity, he added.

Robinson also vehemently denied ever misrepresenting himself to Birthright, by stating that his program was affiliated with the Presbyterian Church of Stanley. He claimed to have merely named his church, when he was asked about his religious affiliations. He also refuted the allegations of offering to pay for a girl to fly to Dallas for job-training, or of ever giving a Christmas deadline for finding a mother and baby for the program.

The tense meeting ended with Haymes saying he would need to contact the Truman Medical Center social workers to substantiate the Kansas City Outreach program. But at Robinson's request he agreed not to identify himself as his probation officer, saying only that Robinson had contacted him to find young mothers on probation for his program. Then Haymes allowed Robinson to telephone Karen Gaddis from his office to warn her to expect his call.

On his way out, Robinson invited his probation officer to visit his Equi-II offices the following week and inspect all the relevant forms and brochures, which he promised to have available. As he swaggered out of the building, he did not seem the least bit concerned about all Haymes' questions on Kansas City Outreach.

After the meeting, Steve Haymes was more convinced than ever that John Robinson was deeply involved in criminal activities. And he resolved to find enough evidence for Judge Hutcherson to revoke probation and send Robinson back to jail.

But the young probation officer had no idea just how dangerous Robinson was, or that he may have already crossed the line over to murder.

The day after the interview Steve Haymes telephoned Karen Gaddis and learned that the Overland Police Department was now investigating the disappearances of Lisa and Tiffany Stasi and their ties to Robinson.

According to Haymes' case notes, the Truman Medical Center social worker said it was "strange" how John Robinson's stories did not add up. Initially Robinson had told her that he'd been referred to Truman Medical Center by Catholic Charities. But then when she'd checked, they had said Robinson had called them, saying Truman Medical Center had referred him.

Even more alarming to Haymes was that Truman Medical Center's social services were now actively using the Kansas City Outreach Program. The hospital had already sent Robinson two young black girls, who were currently staying at his Troost Avenue apartment, although they appeared to be doing well.

"Gaddis cautioned this officer that there was some question about the program as a white girl had disappeared approximately three weeks earlier," reported Haymes. "Detective Cindy Scott and Larry Dixon of the Overland Park Police Department were looking into the situation."

It was a stunning development and sent alarm bells

ringing for the probation officer, who immediately stepped-up his investigation and devoted himself to it full-time.

Steve Haymes then called Robinson's attorney, Ron Wood, to find out what he knew. Wood was aware of Kansas City Outreach, although he admitted he was not financially involved, as he had some questions about the "liability of the situation." He also confirmed that he and Robinson had discussed filing it as a charity, but as yet nothing had been done.

The following morning Steve Haymes called the Overland police department and spoke to Detective Larry Dixon. He confirmed that police were investigating the disappearances of Lisa and Tiffany Stasi, after their family had reported them missing. But so far the only action taken had been to take statements from the Stasi family, as there was "no indication of wrong doing." Detective Dixon said he might assign another detective to work on the case for a few days, if the Stasis did not turn up soon.

Then Dixon mentioned that the Overland Park Police Department had received another call a few months earlier from Bill Godfrey, after his daughter Paula had gone missing. He explained that the police had then received a letter from Paula, saying she was safe and grateful to John Robinson for all his help. Satisfied that the letter was genuine, they had not taken any further action.

Steve Haymes then briefed the detective on his findings and they agreed to keep in close touch with any new developments.

His next call, to Catholic Services, confirmed that some Kansas City social service agencies had more information about John Robinson than others. As a result, Robinson was able to slip through any safety nets. Catholic Services worker Jeannie Bishop told the probation officer that they had been "cautious" about Robinson and had refused to work with him.

"They were aware of information which made them very suspicious," Haymes reported.

Bishop explained how Robinson had first contacted her supervisor, Brian O'Malley, about the Kansas City Outreach Program, claiming to have funding from Xerox and other national corporations. He had also told O'Malley of his affiliation with the First Presbyterian Church of Kansas, who had later denied it when he had called to check. And Bishop was also well aware that Lisa and Tiffany Stasi had gone missing.

That afternoon Haymes drove out to the Truman Medical Center, to interview Karen Gaddis and Sharon Jackson Turner at Hope House. For the next hour, according to Haymes' detailed case notes, he sat transfixed in their office as they told him how they had inadvertently put Lisa and Tiffany Stasi in Robinson's clutches before the troubled young mother and her daughter had gone missing from the Rodeway Inn on January 10, and of the suspicious letters that had arrived soon afterwards.

But Steve Haymes was not a policeman and had few powers outside the court. There was still no real case against Robinson and he would need far stronger evidence that Robinson had breached his Missouri probation order, before Judge Hutcherson could step in and revoke it.

Over the next two months, Haymes interviewed many people associated with Robinson, to build a strong case against him. He met Kathy Klinginsmith and Betty Stasi in their homes, where they told him of their fears for Lisa and Tiffany's safety. And he spoke to Lisa's concerned brother Marty, who revealed Robinson had called his boss at work and tried to get him fired, after he had demanded answers.

He would even try and catch Robinson off-guard, by calling him at all hours with new questions. But, as arrogant as ever, John Robinson always seemed to have an answer for everything. The fact that he was now obviously under investigation did not seem to bother him in the least.

When Steve Haymes arrived at the plush Equi-II offices on January 31, John Robinson was well-prepared. Walking Haymes into his office and inviting him to take a seat, he treated it more as a business meeting than an interview with his probation officer. As Haymes closely observed the office, with its impressive display of medical diplomas on the walls, he quietly noted a sign that Equi-II was a member of the Kansas City Chamber of Commerce. Later, when he checked, the chamber had no record of the company.

The president of Equi-II brimmed with pride as he handed Haymes copies of all the previously requested forms relating to Kansas City Outreach. He even boasted of already setting aside $6,000 of corporate funds to finance the program, adding that he planned to secure additional funding from IBM, Xerox and other interested businessmen, once the program was fully operational. Later when Haymes checked with IBM he was told the corporation does not give money to other organizations.

Haymes then changed tack and asked about Equi-II and what it did. Robinson seemed in his element as he explained it was a business consulting firm, bringing out a collection of glossy booklets and brochures he had prepared for new clients to illustrate his point. He then proceeded to give a lengthy explanation of how his company formed limited partnerships for businessmen involved in the cattle industry.

A week later Haymes was back in Robinson's office

with another probation officer, Bill Neely. This time they were there to question him directly about Lisa and Tiffany's mysterious disappearance.

Totally unruffled, Robinson said they had been sent to him by Karen Gaddis, but he had not been able to accommodate them in his Troost Avenue apartment as it was full. Haymes asked how that could be if it housed three girls, and only two were staying there at present. Parrying the question, Robinson claimed that there were only two beds, so there had been nowhere for them to sleep. Instead he had put the mother and daughter up in the Rodeway Inn, until they could be placed elsewhere.

He told the probation officers how Lisa had once walked out without telling him and he'd finally tracked her down to her relatives in Missouri, where she had gone to spend the night. The next morning he had collected Lisa and Tiffany from her relatives' house during a snowstorm, and brought them back to the Rodeway Inn. When they had arrived at the motel, a man called Bill was waiting for her in the lobby, he claimed.

Wrote Haymes in his report: "He stated that the following morning, Thursday, Stasi and the individual known to him as Bill came to his office and turned over the key to the room at the Rodeway Inn. He states that he has not seen or heard from Stasi since that time."

According to Robinson, he had then gone to the motel and paid the bill with an American Express card, saying it was processed by a clerk named Diana.

Then, for the first time John Robinson became visibly angry with the probation officers. He said he could not understand why everyone was "making such a big deal," as he was only trying to help people, and he threatened to close down the Kansas City Outreach Program.

Haymes then warned him that "there certainly were a

lot of questions being raised" and that he was in "jeopardy," as he was still on probation.

After leaving Equi-II, Haymes and Neely went straight to the Rodeway Inn and spoke to a clerk named Madeline, who remembered Lisa and Tiffany Stasi. She confirmed that Diana did work there but was off-duty. Madeline remembered Lisa Stasi as a good guest, who had not caused any disturbances. But she could not remember the name of the man who paid her bill and had no recollections of any other men visiting the Stasis during their three-day stay.

"She thought that Stasi left with Robinson," wrote Haymes. "To her knowledge Robinson had not had any other people staying at that motel."

Back at his office, Haymes received a call from Karen Gaddis, who reported a strange telephone call she had had with Robinson the previous day. He had called with the news that he was personally "writing a grant" for a new social services position, paying $27,000 a year. He said he thought she would be the perfect candidate for the job and would have a "good chance" if she applied. Then he "pressured" her for another white girl and baby.

On February 21, Johnson County District Attorney Larry McClane called Steve Haymes with some encouraging news. His office was now actively investigating Mildred Amadi's allegation that John Robinson had arranged her bogus divorce. Additionally, he was also examining Robinson and his company in connection with several other serious fraud cases, involving several hundred thousand dollars. He warned Haymes that Robinson would soon be arrested.

CHAPTER 8

THE NET CLOSES

ON Tuesday, March 19, 1985, a visibly nervous Irv Blattner walked into the U.S. Secret Service office in Kansas City, offering to turn government witness and tell them everything he knew about John Robinson's criminal enterprises. Blattner was convinced that his former friend intended to make him the fall guy for illegally cashing a government check. As Blattner was already on two years' probation himself for bad checks, and faced prison, he offered to testify against Robinson.

A week earlier, Robinson had been questioned by the Secret Service under oath about a $741 government check, which had been illegally cashed by a friend of his, Brenda Harris (not her real name). Pleading total innocence, he claimed that Blattner had arrived at his office the previous June with the unsigned check, asking him to cash it. He had refused, saying he wanted nothing to do with it.

Now Blattner was eager to tell Special Agent John Guerber his version of events, agreeing to testify if it came to trial. According to Blattner, Robinson had attended a business meeting at the Midwest College of Medical Assistants, the Equi-II client where he worked in administration. After the meeting Robinson had walked into his office and spotted an unsigned $741 Veterans Administration check for a student named James Hargrove, issued by the U.S. Treasury.

When Robinson demanded the check, Blattner refused, saying it was not signed by Hargrove or endorsed over to the school. Refusing to take no for an answer,

Robinson had spent the next month pressuring him for the check. Eventually, after Robinson threatened to have him fired from the job he had found him, Blattner gave him the unsigned check and was promised $200 commission.

The next day Robinson called him in a panic, claiming that his friend Brenda Harris had taken the check to a bank, but it had been flagged as stolen. The teller had then refused to cash it, making a photocopy before returning the check to Harris. Robinson then said he had destroyed the check.

Earlier, Harris had told Agent Guerber an entirely different version in a sworn statement. She claimed Robinson had telephoned her at home, saying he had a check he wanted her to cash, and that she could make some money.

She then drove to Equi-II where Robinson gave her the check, which had already been signed. He wanted $600 in cash for it, saying she could keep the rest. Harris agreed to his terms and drove straight to the Clay County State Bank in Claycomo, Missouri, where her brother-in-law worked as a teller. He cashed the stolen check with no questions asked, taking $20 for his services and giving Brenda $721 in cash. She kept $121 as agreed, mailing Robinson the remaining $600.

Straight after Robinson's interview with the Secret Service office, he called Blattner, warning him that "We're in deep trouble." Then he instructed him to give false testimony at his upcoming interview with Guerber.

Under Robinson's elaborate alibi, Blattner was to say that he had sold a riding lawnmower to someone claiming to be James Hargrove, who had paid with a check. When he came to cash the check he had lost his ID and asked Robinson to do it as a favor.

This was the tangled set of circumstances that led

Blattner to turn on Robinson and offer to testify against him for the government.

Guerber was very interested in what Blattner had to say about the mysterious Robinson, whom he was well aware of. There were other matters that he also wanted to discuss. First he asked Blattner if Robinson had impersonated an attorney during Mildred Amadi's illegal divorce.

Blattner admitted he had first introduced his former tenant to John Robinson, but maintained that he did not know whether Robinson had posed as an attorney. He told the special agent that Amadi had married a Nigerian in a marriage of convenience so he could remain in the country. He had mentioned her plight to Robinson, who said he knew an attorney who could help her with a divorce.

Special Agent Guerber then asked if Robinson had ever mentioned any organization that helped young mothers and babies. Blattner remembered them once discussing an idea to set up a home for young pregnant girls. Robinson's plan was to find a home out in the country without any "communication or transportation," and have the girls stay there until they gave birth. Then he would put the babies up for adoption.

Blattner said Robinson already had two doctors to give the girls daily health checks and had hired a lawyer to prepare the necessary adoption papers for the girls to sign. But he claimed he had refused to get involved in the adoption scheme, and it was never discussed again.

At the end of the meeting, Blattner gave a signed statement to the Secret Service implicating John Robinson in a number of illegal activities. Within twenty-four hours the Clay County Court in Missouri had issued a warrant for his arrest for probation violations, setting a bond for a hundred thousand dollars.

* * *

At 11:55 a.m. on Thursday, March 21, John Robinson was arrested when he arrived at Steve Haymes' office for a probation meeting. When Haymes told him there was an outstanding warrant for his arrest, Robinson calmly called his attorney and agreed to surrender.

As Haymes drove him to the Clay County Jail, Robinson casually mentioned that Lisa and Tiffany Stasi had now been found. He claimed that his office had received a call from Patricia Grant (not her real name) one of the mothers in Robinson's Kansas City Outreach Program, who was looking for Stasi so she could pay her for some baby-sitting.

"According to Robinson this girl said Stasi [and her daughter] were with a guy who she had known for some time," Haymes would later write in his probation report. "Robinson stated that this girl knew nicknames and that he was convinced that Stasi was still around and everything was fine." Patricia also claimed Lisa had told her that she wanted no further contact with her family.

Robinson told his probation officer that he had instructed Patricia to contact his attorney, Ron Wood, who had then called the Overland Park Police Department with the good news. Everything, he assured Haymes, had already been verified by Detective Cindy Scott.

As Robinson posted a $50,000 bond later that day and was released from custody, Scott and FBI Agent Tom Lavin interviewed Patricia. At first she confirmed everything Robinson had said, but Lavin, who was now working the case for the prostitution and baby-selling angles, was highly suspicious. To try to catch her out, Detective Scott showed Patricia a photograph of a young female, asking if it was Lisa Stasi. Without hesitation Patricia said it was, but on being told it was someone else, she broke down and agreed to tell them the truth.

"She was told to tell this story by Robinson," Haymes would later report, "as she owed him $900 and he had taken nude pictures of her."

Patricia then admitted that she had never met Lisa Stasi or her baby daughter.

The day after his release Robinson decided to punish Irv Blattner for cooperating with the Secret Service. He called Haymes, saying Blattner had contacted him and wanted to borrow money, intimating that it could be blackmail. He said he had arranged with his attorney to record the conversation and do whatever was necessary to prove that he was not guilty of these alleged violations.

Blattner was also running scared after receiving a furious letter from Robinson, accusing him of "betrayal." Terrified that his former friend, whom he secretly suspected of killing Paula Godfrey, might try and injure him, Blattner told several close friends to contact the FBI if anything were to happen to him. He also carefully hid Robinson's letter, along with the one-page Paula note, in a trunk at his house as further insurance.

That afternoon Steve Haymes was briefed by Agent Lavin, who now had strong evidence that Equi-II's Troost Avenue apartment fronted as a brothel. Lavin had discovered that Brenda Harris, who had cashed the Hargrove check, had been asked by Robinson to become a prostitute for him and had run into some other girls, who were already working there. Lavin also told Haymes that Robinson had asked the two young mothers in his Kansas City Outreach Program to become prostitutes.

After the FBI briefing, an astonished Haymes called Karen Gaddis to tell her that the girls Truman Medical Center had sent to Troost Avenue were in moral danger. According to Haymes' notes, Gaddis said they had been advised to move out as it was "a bad situation," but, they being "street people" and it being a nice apartment, they were reluctant to. Haymes advised the social worker to get "that acknowledgment" in writing and ask them again to move.

An hour later Gaddis called Haymes with some terrifying news. Within the last two weeks Robinson had contacted another Kansas City maternity home called the White House, looking for more pregnant young girls for his program. She also mentioned that Agent Lavin had asked her to "string" Robinson along if he called again about the job.

Four days later, on Tuesday, March 26, John Robinson and his attorney, Bruce Houdek—who had represented him during his 1982 securities fraud case—arrived at the Missouri State Probation Office for a parole violation interview. It would formally address three alleged counts of parole violation, which would then go into the official report that Haymes was preparing for Judge Hutcherson of the Clay County Court.

In the first count, regarding Mildred Amadi's divorce, Robinson denied ever representing himself as a divorce lawyer, receiving money and her car for his services, or ever telling her she was divorced. He said that Amadi would testify to this in court. But Haymes already knew that only the day before Robinson had telephoned Amadi, saying he knew a lawyer who would process her divorce properly, and offering to pay for the services.

As to the second count, of forgery and cashing James Hargrove's check, Robinson stuck by his statement to the Secret Service, again claiming that Irv Blattner had first brought it to his office.

On the third alleged parole violation, of consorting with someone with a criminal record, Robinson denied knowing that Blattner was on probation. He said he was aware that Blattner had had "problems with a check," but said he had loaned his friend money to try and help him out.

"Robinson is continuing to involve himself in criminal activity," Haymes wrote in his official report. "Robinson has been involved in criminal activity for over fifteen years and, to date, has managed to obtain probation when caught, but never required to serve a significant period of incarceration."

After leaving Haymes' office, Robinson returned to Equi-II and immediately called Karen Gaddis. He announced that he was applying for a grant with the Ford Foundation and needed Truman Medical Center to provide letters of reference within three days. He also wanted letters from the two girls, adding that he was now talking to the Social Rehabilitation Services in Kansas. Gaddis said she would see what she could do and called Haymes for advice.

Haymes told her to go ahead and write a carefully-worded letter of reference, stating that there was a need for such a program, but not in any way intimating that Robinson was a "great guy." He warned her to prepare to be subpoened when Robinson eventually went to court to "show he is a con man."

Some years later Haymes would sum up the frustrations of being Robinson's probation officer, saying: "He never gives up. Most people, you catch them in a lie . . . It'll shut them down. He's like one of those toys that runs into a wall and goes on. The game was everything to him."

When Agent Lavin heard that Robinson was still actively seeking young pregnant women to move into Troost Avenue, he considered sending a young female agent undercover to infiltrate Kansas City Outreach. But before the plan could be implemented, the FBI got their big break, when John Robinson recruited another young woman into prostitution.

CHAPTER 9

ARMED AND DANGEROUS

THERESA L. Williams arrived in Kansas City in 1984 to start a new life. The pretty teenager soon found part-time work, doing odd jobs at Russell's Laundry on East-wood Trafficway and at the local Kmart next door. But the pay was bad and she found it hard to make ends meet.

In late April 1985, Williams met John Robinson at a McDonald's, after he struck up a conversation with her. The friendly, slightly balding stranger soon put her at ease, asking her about herself and where she worked. When she told him about her struggle to survive, work-ing two menial jobs, he immediately offered her a way out. He told her she was an attractive woman and he knew how she could make big money easily.

"He said he could take care of me," Williams would later testify in Clay County Circuit Court, "and I wouldn't have to worry about working, about anything."

A couple of weeks earlier Karen Gaddis had finally persuaded the two young mothers to move out of the Troost Avenue apartment, which was now vacant. Rob-inson, who had been considering letting it go, invited Williams to move in and let him become her pimp, and she agreed.

Two weeks after she moved in, Robinson arrived one night with half a bag of marijuana for her. He also started bringing around men who were willing to pay well for her sexual favors.

On one occasion, Williams told investigators, Rob-inson arranged for her to have a sado-masochistic sexual encounter with a rich Kansas City businessman, for which she would receive $1,200.

"He was a certain man who needed brutality and who paid for it," she would later explain to the FBI.

During the session, Williams was blindfolded and placed in the back of her client's limousine to have "unnatural sex acts," while they were driven around Kansas City by his chauffeur. She was then paid off by the driver and dropped off in the street.

During her two months at Troost Avenue, John Robinson was a frequent visitor. She noticed that he always carried a pistol in a shoulder holster underneath his business suit, and could become violent at times. There was one terrifying incident, soon after she moved in, that would haunt her for years. Late one night, fast asleep in her bedroom, she awoke to find Robinson standing menacingly over her bed, with a strange look in his eyes.

"He woke me up and started pulling my hair," she would tearfully remember. "I started screaming. And then he took the gun out, put it to my head, and said, 'If you don't shut up, I'll blow your brains out.' " Then, according to her sworn testimony, Robinson stuck the gun barrel in her vagina and sexually assaulted her with it.

During her stay at the apartment Robinson also recruited her into a sinister scheme to apparently frame Irv Blattner for her murder, in order to discredit his testimony in his upcoming probation revocation hearing. Robinson began dictating a daily diary for her to transcribe in her own handwriting, that pointed the finger straight at Blattner if anything were to happen to her. The fictitious diary's final entry was to be June 15, 1985.

Under his direction she wrote that she was in fear of her life, giving Robinson's attorney detailed instructions to receive the diary, and some property that she had in a safe-deposit box, if something were to happen to her.

The date of the last entry is chillingly significant. Williams would later tell FBI investigators that on June 14 she was to leave with Robinson on a Bahamas vacation, after they had put her belongings into storage.

A couple of days before Theresa Williams believed she was going to the Bahamas, the FBI moved in and probably saved her life. Agent Tom Lavin and his partner, Agent Jeffery Dancer, had had the Troost Avenue apartment under close surveillance for several months. Now they decided to make their move.

One morning, while Williams was at a self-service laundry near the apartment, the two agents arrived to question her about John Robinson. She told them about the two months she had spent as Robinson's prostitute, mentioning that he was armed, and that he was about to take her on a vacation to the Bahamas.

Realizing they had to get her away from Robinson immediately, they took her straight back to the apartment, helped her pack her things and then moved her into a safe house. They moved so fast that they accidentally took a TV set belonging to Robinson's landlord.

"The agents felt I was in danger," she would later testify.

When John Robinson returned to the apartment later that day and found her missing without a trace, he was livid. For the next three weeks he scoured the streets of Kansas City in a desperate attempt to find her.

The two FBI agents and Steve Haymes debriefed Theresa Williams on June 18 and were shocked by her story of how Robinson had led her into drugs and prostitution. The FBI felt she was in such peril while Robinson remained free, that she was given around-the-clock protection at a safe house at 3241 College Boulevard,

Kansas City. Over the next few weeks the FBI would move Williams to three different safe houses to ensure that Robinson did not find her.

"It appears that Robinson is continuing to be involved in shaky and criminal activities and that he is continuing to manipulate away any responsibilities for his actions," wrote Haymes in a mid-June report to Judge Hutcherson. "It further appears that he has continued to use people to his own end, including Ms. Williams with whom there is concern for her safety, as brought to question by the contents of the diary."

At the beginning of July, John Robinson hired Kansas City private detective Charles H. Lane, through his attorney Bruce Houdek, to find Theresa Williams. The former policeman with the Johnson County Sheriff's Department had more than twenty years' law enforcement experience, but ultimately it would be Robinson and his wife Nancy who finally tracked down Theresa.

By July 8, Robinson had narrowed down the safe house to within a three-block radius of College Boulevard and ordered Lane to start searching house-to-house. The following morning he went out at 4:00 a.m. but was unable to find her.

Two days later Robinson called to inform him that he and Nancy had been driving around the area and had identified Williams' car in the carport at 3241 College Boulevard.

"On July eleventh, I also located Theresa L. Williams' car and confirmed the license number of the auto," Lane later testified on Robinson's behalf, to persuade Judge Hutcherson that he did not pose any threat to her. "[Four days later], I contacted the landlady at the address and confirmed that Theresa L. Williams did in fact live at this address with a black male whose name is Bradley Vaughn. I was also informed by the landlady that this same day two men dressed in suits had come by and picked [her] up. The landlady stated that she was told they were going to take her and help her find a job."

A week later Lane went back to the safe house and found Williams there. But as he was talking to the girl, FBI Agents Lavin and Dancer arrived and ordered him to leave.

"They told me they were FBI, but did not show their identification," said Lane. "Theresa L. Williams, who had been talking to me, decided not to continue our conversation."

After the private detective's hasty departure, the two special agents were so concerned Robinson now knew her location, that they arranged to have the probation service give her $350 in cash and a plane ticket out of town.

"We felt after talking to [Williams] about the things he had demanded and the things he had done to her, it was necessary to keep her away from him," Lavin would later explain. "We shipped her out of the city."

They were so concerned for her safety that they even defied a court order to return her to Kansas City to give a deposition, refusing to reveal her whereabouts at a hearing to revoke Robinson's probation.

The Monday after Williams was put on a plane to an unknown destination, Agents Lavin and Dancer gave guarded depositions to Clay County Court. Steve Haymes gave his a couple of days later. They all refused to produce notes of their interview with Theresa Williams or even say where it had taken place. And they also wouldn't reveal what she had said about Robinson's involvement with guns, drugs and prostitution.

Agent Lavin also refused to explain to the court why the FBI had felt Williams to be in such great danger.

"There is no rational reason why the State and the

agents cannot produce Theresa Williams at the courthouse for her deposition," complained Robinson's attorney Bruce Houdek in a motion to the court.

On July 19, Judge John R. Hutcherson, also concerned for Williams' safety, ruled that the agents would
not have to produce her in court or disclose where she
was hidden. Years later Judge Hutcherson, now retired
from the bench, would explain: "I wasn't going to let
[Robinson] have that address."

Ten days later John Robinson returned to Clay
County Circuit Court for a two-day hearing which found
he had violated his 1981 probation on three counts. The
hearing was then adjourned for three weeks to allow the
court to decide whether to send him back to prison to
serve out his original seven-year sentence.

"It would appear from this behavior that Robinson has
little regard for the conditions of probation," wrote Steve
Haymes.

Now, in a final attempt to try to sway Judge Hutcherson's verdict in his favor, John Robinson embarked on
a public relations campaign, portraying himself as a
valuable civic asset. He commissioned a private marketing company to prepare a glossy brochure for the
judge, outlining his voluntary work and many good
deeds in the community.

"Mr. Robinson and his wife have always been involved in community activities," said the report, adding
that Robinson was "an honest and generous person." The
report also lauded Robinson for being an elder at the
Presbyterian Church of Stanley and teaching Sunday
school.

Among his many achievements listed in the report
was scouting, although it failed to mention that the Boy
Scouts of America had officially removed Robinson as
a Scoutmaster after his conviction for stealing from

Guy's Foods, refusing to renew his membership after the trial.

It also included a forged letter to the court from a fictitious unemployed pregnant mother of three named Linda White, thanking Robinson and his family for their altruism over the previous Christmas.

"On Christmas Eve, Mr. Robinson and his children brought boxes of things over to the house," read the typed letter bearing the childlike signature of the non-existent Linda White. "There were socks, underwear and clothes for all the kids, and food for Christmas Day and enough for a week later. I had my baby in January and because of the help and encouragement I received from Mr. Robinson and his wife, I decided to keep my baby."

But Robinson's extraordinary attempts to influence the judge had little effect. On August 21, Judge Hutcherson revoked John Robinson's probation and ordered him to serve seven years at the Missouri Department of Corrections. The judge also refused to grant Robinson's request for a stay of execution. But two days later, Judge Hutcherson did allow Robinson to remain free on $250,000 bail while he appealed the sentence, setting strict conditions that he report to Steve Haymes' office once a day between Monday and Friday, and check in by phone on the weekends. He was also ordered not to contact Theresa Williams or any other state witnesses involved in his case.

But ultimately Robinson triumphed over the legal system once again when, in May 1986, the Missouri Court of Appeals reversed Judge Hutcherson's decision, ordering a new hearing to revoke Robinson's probation. Appeals Judge David J. Dixon ruled that Robinson's constitutional rights had been violated, as he hadn't been allowed to confront Theresa Williams in court.

"There cannot be the least doubt that the actions of

the probation service and the FBI agents denied petitioner due process of law," wrote Judge Dixon in his ruling.

Although John Robinson had managed to manipulate the courts and remain out of jail, his days of freedom were numbered, as the ongoing criminal investigations into Equi-II and his questionable business practices all came to a head.

CHAPTER 10

THE SCALES OF JUSTICE

A few days after John Robinson's first probation hearing he was in the spotlight again, this time portraying himself as an innovative businessman. He even made the cover of the August 1985 edition of the national trade magazine *Farm Journal*, where Equi-II was the subject of a six-page feature in the Beef Extra supplement, headlined: "Is a Limited Partnership in Your Future?"

The *Farm Journal* editors, who were unaware of Robinson's criminal record, assigned a writer to interview him for the extensive feature, in which he advised farmers on the tax benefits of limited partnerships, sounding every inch the expert financial consultant.

"For every dollar the limited partner invests, he gets $2 to $4 in tax write-offs, along with a return of 25 percent to 50 percent on his investment over the life of the partnership," declared Robinson.

He even boasted of Equi-II's business acumen, telling the *Farm Journal* readers of a groundbreaking $2.2 million partnership he had recently set up for a client, which would revolutionize the farm industry. Sounding like a captain of industry, the Equi-II president pointed out that the more the client makes for investors, "the more he takes home."

Robinson's interview ran alongside ones from such distinguished experts as Sam Brownback, at the time an Agricultural Law Professor at Kansas State University and now a U.S. senator, who discussed the advantages of limited partnerships to beef farmers.

Indeed he was so impressive in the article that at least

three farmers considered investing in Equi-II, until they contacted the Johnson County District Attorney's Office and were told of Robinson's criminal record. But other, less fortunate ones, like Kansas rancher Bob Lowrey and his partner Bill Mills, who each invested $10,000 in Equi-II, lost all their money.

"We never saw anything come out of all the talk," Lowrey would later tell *The Kansas City Star*. "I questioned it at the time, but Billy did visit with the man [and] was certain he was an honest person."

Despite all his legal problems in late 1985, John Robinson still seemed to thrive. He moved Equi-II into a smart new second-floor suite of offices at the corner of College Boulevard and Knoll in Overland Park, seeming impervious to all the criminal cases pending against him.

His son John Jr., now a student at Kansas University, had given him the idea to publish a university sports magazine, so he began looking for advertising sponsors. He placed an advertisement in *The Kansas City Star* for experienced salespeople, which was answered by Phil Spell.

"I met John two or three times and all we talked about was business," remembers Spell, who was working for Southwestern Bell Yellow Pages and looking for a new job. "He had all these ideas and seemed like an entrepreneur. I thought at the time his job was intriguing, but I didn't think it would fly in the real world."

After turning down the position, Spell recommended a Southwestern Bell colleague named Richard Clinton, who ended up becoming Equi-II's new sales manager.

"He was a good con man," said Clinton in hindsight. "It all sounded very good. He seemed a very busy type and had all these things going on."

A few weeks after Clinton began working for Equi-II, Robinson announced that he was taking his family off on a European vacation, and leaving him in charge. He told Clinton he would be checking in from time to time and did not leave any contact numbers.

One morning while he was away a female colleague asked Clinton to meet her for coffee, saying she had some important information about their boss.

"She had all the scoop on him," said Clinton. "She knew what a crook he was."

When Clinton heard that his employer had a long criminal record and was facing prison, he made some quick calls and soon found a new job. He then summoned the other five Equi-II staff into his office and informed them of Robinson's history, inviting them to come and work for him.

Within the hour, the complete Equi-II staff had resigned, pushing the key through the office door and walking out. During the six weeks Clinton was on Robinson's payroll, he never received a cent, except $150 in traveling expenses a few months later, when he swore out a deposition against his former boss.

When Robinson returned from Amsterdam, he arrived at the Equi-II offices to find the front door locked and his staff gone. He was furious, telephoning Clinton and threatening to sue him for ruining his business.

"The more he talked the madder he became," said Clinton. "Then he threatened to kill me. I told him I was an army veteran and if anyone does any killing, I would."

Then Clinton drove to the Johnson County Courthouse in Olathe, and complained to Assistant District Attorney Steve Obermeier that Robinson had threatened his life.

At the beginning of 1986, John Robinson's luck was about to run out as a series of separate criminal investigations, on both sides of the Kansas–Missouri border, finally came to court. After nearly five years of evading justice, Robinson would now be overwhelmed by the sheer weight of evidence against him. Finally, Steve Haymes' patient and persistent pursuit of Robinson would pay off.

For months the Johnson County District Attorney's office had been investigating Robinson for cheating Equi-II client Back Care Systems International out of thousands of dollars of falsified expenses. The company had hired Robinson in 1982 to market its innovative new program of staging backache seminars for industrial workers. As part of their contract Equi-II was to prepare a marketing plan, video and slide presentations and printed materials.

But soon Back Care Systems began getting suspicious invoices for work that had not been carried out. The company's owner, Roy Spradlin, had then taken the invoices to Equi-II and asked Robinson to supply paid bills and check numbers to authenticate them.

To cover himself Robinson pressured Irv Blattner to pose as a freelance sound and video technician and supply the relevant signed invoices. In 1985 Blattner told prosecutors that he had forged several invoices totaling $1,630 for video work, studio rental time and sound dubbing a year earlier. Robinson had even had him sign a notarized false affidavit in May 1984, when Back Care Systems had once again questioned the expenses.

"[I] felt compelled to grant the favor," Blattner testified, adding that his former friend had again threatened to have him fired from his job.

On January 30, 1986, following a three-day trial, a jury found John Robinson guilty of felony theft, involving a total of $3,600 in false invoices to Back Care Systems.

Johnson County Assistant D.A. Steve Obermeier, who prosecuted the case, requested that County District Judge Herbert W. Walton activate the Habitual Criminal Act in sentencing Robinson, in view of all his previous convictions. Judge Walton agreed, sentencing him to a prison term of five to fourteen years and ordering him to pay a $5,000 fine.

Robinson's attorneys, James L. Eisenbrandt and Charles Droege, immediately appealed the decision, but their motion to overturn it was denied.

Six months later, on July 10, Robinson was charged with four more counts of fraud and deception by Johnson County District Court. In 1984 he had cold-called Overland Park businessman Gerhard Kuti with an offer to become an investor in a hotel/condominium development on land owned by a wealthy cattle baron in Page, Arizona. He told Kuti he was acting as a middle man, assuring him the property was totally free of debt and offering him a quarter stake in the project for $150,000.

He told Kuti that it was such a good opportunity that he had even taken a quarter share in it himself. Kuti then agreed to become an investor, transferring a personal check for $150,000 to Equi-II, who then mailed him a copy of the sales agreement.

Soon afterwards the owners of the property, Jack and Angialea Goode—who were paying Robinson a $55,000 retainer to find investors—informed Kuti that the property had a $700,000 mortgage on it, expressing surprise that Robinson had failed to mention it. Becoming suspicious, Kuti had Jack Goode send him his copy of the sale agreement which showed that Kuti had actually paid $100,000 for his share, $50,000 less than he had given Robinson. It was obvious that Robinson had deviously switched a page in Kuti's agreement and then doctored the figures.

When he was confronted by the outraged investor, Robinson readily admitted pocketing the $50,000, saying that he had considered it his commission on the deal, on top of the $25,000 agreed commission he received from Goode. Later it was discovered that Robinson had never invested in the property, or revealed his past criminal record, or prior history with the Securities and Exchange Commission.

Eventually, after months of legal wrangling, Robinson was convicted of making a false writing. As a habitual offender, he now faced a total of six to nineteen years in prison at his upcoming sentencing.

Amazingly, Equi-II still managed to survive into 1987 despite a hard-hitting exposé in the Kansas City *Business Journal* in March 1986, detailing Robinson's prodigious sixteen-year career as a white-collar criminal.

"Apparently, Robinson has developed a convincing manner of gaining the confidence of business people over the years," wrote the *Journal*'s Delbert Schafer. "He has the ability to ferret out information and then use it to tell the listener exactly what he wants to hear." A former unidentified business partner told the *Journal* that: "On first meeting, Robinson is completely convincing."

Even with the entire legal systems of two states bearing down on him, John Robinson remained confident he would never go to jail. He still maintained a lavish lifestyle at his home in Pleasant Valley, although his neighbors all knew of his criminal past and did their best to avoid him.

Amazingly, throughout all his legal troubles, his wife Nancy stayed loyal, and was one of his staunchest supporters, accompanying him to numerous attorney meetings and helping strategize his defense. Exactly how much she knew of her husband's criminal activities remains a mystery, and she would never be charged in any of his crimes.

"She was very supportive of John," said Robinson's attorney Bruce Houdek. "They worked together to help him defend himself, pay his fees and provide records and information [for the defense]."

At Pleasant Valley the Robinson family acted as if nothing was amiss. Their eldest children, John Jr., now twenty-one, and Kimberly, eighteen, both went to college at Kansas State, and the twins, Christy and Christopher, were sixteen years old and still attended high school.

Every morning John Robinson would dress up in one of his smart business suits and drive into the Equi-II office, where most of his time was now spent appealing his convictions. But he was still busy recruiting new female staff.

In early 1987, he placed an advertisement in a local paper for a secretary. The high-paying job sounded extremely attractive, with a lot of traveling and even a new wardrobe.

When Catherine Clampitt saw the ad one morning at breakfast, she immediately called Equi-II to set up a job interview. Although her foster brother Robert Bales was suspicious, thinking it sounded "far-fetched," Catherine was hired by Equi-II, and was soon traveling all over the country on unspecified Robinson business.

Born in Korea on May 29, 1960, Catherine had come to America as a child and been adopted by Bales' mother, who lived in Wichita Falls, Texas. But the pretty, petite girl had a "wild side" and got mixed up in a bad crowd, using drugs and alcohol.

In late January 1987, her foster family decided that

she should leave Wichita Falls and make a fresh start away from temptation in Overland Park, Kansas. She would live with Robert Bales and his wife, but her one-year-old baby son Ryan would remain in Wichita Falls, to be looked after by her foster parents.

On a cold January night, Robert Bales met Catherine at the Kansas City bus station and spent the next few days lining up job interviews for her. Within a few days she had been hired by Equi-II as an administrative assistant.

Robinson soon put Clampitt on the road, flying her all over America on his assignments, during which she would often stay at local hotels for several nights at a time. Then in the spring she went missing. Bales immediately suspected John Robinson was somehow involved as he had warned Catherine originally that the job sounded too good to be true.

Catherine Clampitt was officially declared a missing person by the Overland Park Police Department on June 15. But after detectives questioned Robinson they dropped the case, saying there was not enough evidence against him to proceed.

Then Bales started his own investigation. For the next few months he kept calling the Equi-II offices for news on Catherine and once even staked out John Robinson, looking for leads. Hoping to reactivate the police investigation, he compiled a complete dossier of receipts, pictures and everything he had concerning his missing sister.

"He knew I was looking for her," Bales would later tell *The Kansas City Star*.

Clampitt's family all knew the devoted young mother would never abandon her young son. But as the years went by they resigned themselves to the fact that she was probably dead and moved on with their lives.

CHAPTER II

A MODEL PRISONER

ON May 16, 1987, soon after Catherine Clampitt disappeared, John Robinson surrendered to the Johnson County Jail in Olathe, to begin serving a minimum sentence of five years. He was then transferred to the Kansas State Penitentiary in Hutchinson, as the Missouri authorities began the paperwork to ensure that, after completing his sentence in Kansas, he would be transported across state lines to face a further seven years' incarceration for violating probation.

A week later *The Kansas City Star* printed a two-page story on the forty-three-year-old disgraced businessman, headlined: "Kansas Prison Awaiting a Convincing Talker."

"He is headed to a state penitentiary for the first time in his criminal career, which is nearly as long as some of his fellow inmates are old," began the article. "[He] is a thief, a charmer, a skilled conversationalist and a crafty con artist who should have been locked away years ago.

"Only now, eighteen years after his first conviction, is the Johnson County businessman seeing the scales of justice crash down, ending a compulsion for white-collar crime that some authorities say they think may have had a darker side."

Now, for the first time in print, Robinson was linked to the disappearances of Lisa and Tiffany Stasi, although there was no mention of Paula Godfrey, and it would be another two weeks before Catherine Clampitt would be officially reported missing.

Johnson County Assistant D.A. Steve Obermeier told the *Star* that Robinson had benefited from courts being lax on white-collar crime. Even Robinson's own attorney, Bruce Houdek, who to this day denies ever suspecting a violent streak in his "honest" client, now described him as "arrogant and aggressive."

Soon after her husband was sent to prison, Nancy Robinson found a nursing job and put their Pleasant Valley house on the market, as she could no longer afford to make the payments. Her eldest two children had left home and she had to support the twins, Christy and Christopher.

The years of expensive legal battles had finally taken their toll and the Robinsons were left almost penniless, facing many thousands of dollars of damages in pending civil suits. That month Robinson applied for legal aid and gave a financial affidavit, claiming his previous year's income had only been $24,000. Out of that he said he paid $786 a month mortgage and $400 to feed and clothe his family. He wrote that at present there was "no income for family now that I am in Jail."

In January 1988, Nancy sold the family house to Gene Clark and moved into a cheaper apartment in Stanley, Kansas, with the twins. A few months later Scott Davis, who says he never harbored any ill will against Nancy for what her husband had done to his family, decided to visit her with his mother, to see if she was all right.

"The kids answered and I asked to see Nancy," said Davis, "but she just never came out."

Hutchinson Correctional Facility dates back to 1885 when the Kansas legislature appropriated $1 million to build a new facility for first-time youthful offenders. There was much competition from neighboring Kansas cities and towns to build the new state-of-the-art prison, which would bring employment and economic prosperity to the western half of the state.

Eventually the city of Hutchinson, which lies about two hundred miles southwest of Kansas City, was selected after the city council raised $25,000 and offered a choice of two sites to house the prison. Among the chief fundraisers was a rather dubious group called the Hutchinson Ladies Circle—a group of prostitutes operating within the city limits—who raised $1,000 for the project, claiming they liked the idea of separating youths from the adult prison population.

On hearing the news that Hutchinson had been selected as the site for the state's new reformatory, a public holiday was declared and the day-long celebrations included a fireworks display.

Constructed of Hutchinson brick, made from clay dug out of the Arkansas River, the prison consisted of three cell blocks surrounded by a twenty-foot-high wall.

By the time John Robinson entered Hutchinson it was long past its glory days as a model penitentiary. He was assigned as a medium security prisoner in the new South Unit, housing 160 inmates, which had been completed two years earlier.

Soon after arriving the new inmate visited the prison doctor, saying that he suffered from chest pains caused by angina, and requesting medication. After checking with his M.D. back in Kansas he was prescribed a daily dose of nitroglycerin and Tenomin.

Right from the very beginning of his sentence, Inmate #45690 was an exemplary prisoner, who determined to make the best use of his time behind bars. Before long the prison authorities had recognized his intelligence, appointing him to the gravy job of office coordinator for the jail's maintenance operation.

So ironically, under the guidance of the Kansas Penal

System, he first learned about computers and had soon made himself indispensable. Within a few months he had reorganized the maintenance office, becoming an expert in writing new software programs and saving the state an estimated $100,000 annually. His prison supervisor, Jim Jestes, was so delighted with Robinson that in a 1989 report he noted: "Even when he leaves, this office should function well."

But even behind bars, Inmate Robinson was still gunning for his enemies outside. In April he summoned Detective Jerry Burke to his cell, saying he had important information about the selling of cocaine in Kansas City. After a cursory investigation, the detective concluded that Robinson had been lying. Robinson soon recanted his story, admitting a charge of falsely reporting a crime, pleading *nolo contendere*. He was fined $1,000, given an additional 270 days on top of his sentence and ordered to continue his psychiatric counseling until his release.

On July 21, 1989, Robinson's father, Henry Sr., died at the age of seventy-three in Cicero. His mother Alberta would die a few years later after a long, painful illness. His father's funeral was attended by his two brothers, Henry Jr. and Donald and his sisters Jo Ann and Mary Ellen.

According to his obituary in the *Chicago Tribune*, the Robinson patriarch left a total of ten grandchildren, including Donald Robinson's five-year-old adopted daughter, Heather, who was now being brought up as a member of the family. Although John Robinson couldn't attend, as he was behind bars, the family would cite little Heather as one of the few good deeds he had ever done for them.

Soon after his father's death, the forty-five-year-old inmate suffered a series of strokes that briefly hospitalized him, leaving permanent neurological damage. The right side of his face was partially paralyzed with "slackness," noted Dr. Ky Hoang, the Director of Medical Services at the Kansas Department of Corrections, who prepared a medical evaluation of him in January 1990. Dr. Hoang measured Robinson's verbal skills in the "high average range" and his "performance skills in the very superior range."

Wrote Dr. Hoang in his glowing report: "During the course of his incarceration, Mr. Robinson's behavior has been remarkable. He is considered a model inmate who is cooperative and willing to participate."

The report recommended that Robinson should be freed on parole immediately with "no unusual terms or conditions," as he has "shown concrete signs of rehabilitation. He is a docile, non-violent individual who does not pose a threat to society. It is unlikely that further incarceration will be of any benefit to either Mr. Robinson or society."

But his old nemesis, Missouri probation officer Steve Haymes, suspecting that yet again Robinson was pulling the wool over everyone's eyes, doubled his efforts to ensure that Robinson would stay behind bars in Missouri.

On January 23, 1991, John Robinson was officially paroled by the state of Kansas and was handed over to the Missouri prison authorities to begin serving the time he owed them. He was transported over state lines to Moberly Correctional Center, one hundred miles east of Kansas City, where all new male inmates go for diagnostic assessment.

Only a week earlier the Circuit Court of Clay County had revoked his probation in Missouri, ordering him to serve a seven-year sentence, with a year off for probation already served. He would now be eligible for parole in June 1994 at the earliest, with time off for good behavior.

Now facing a further three years in jail, John Robinson began a campaign to persuade his doctors that he ought to be paroled immediately for ill health. The four years he'd served in Kansas had taken their toll on Robinson, whose thinning hair had turned gray. But his mug shot, taken on his arrival at Moberly, shows he still had not lost his arrogant smirk of superiority.

In view of his medical history of strokes, Robinson was taken to the University of Missouri Medical Center as an emergency case, where he was examined and treated. Then Inmate #177866 was returned to Moberly to start his sentence.

In his medical report the following month, the Missouri Medical Center's Staff Physician, Dr. Fred L. King, described Robinson as a very sick man.

"He exhibited signs of stroke," wrote Dr. King, "including weakness and increased reflexes in his right arm and marked dilation of his left pupil."

Dr. King said his patient would need "a large variety of medication" and thought it inevitable he would have more strokes, even with the finest medical care.

"The prognosis for long life must be guarded due to the seriousness of his vascular disease," wrote Dr. King. "Perhaps his medical condition should be considered in any parole hearing he has."

Three months later, Dr. King again examined Robinson and found him in such a bad condition that he recommended he "should be released without delay," saying his condition was now "life threatening."

When probation officer Steve Haymes read Dr. King's report he was furious, believing that yet again Robinson was trying to manipulate the system to his own ends. He then wrote his own report to the court and testified at a parole hearing in April, when the Missouri Parole Board denied Robinson's petition to be freed on medical grounds, ordering him to serve out his sentence.

A month later John Robinson stepped up his campaign to get out of jail. He wrote an impassioned letter to Clay County Circuit Court Judge Mahoney, pleading for immediate release, as he was under "a sentence of death." Portraying himself as an unfortunate victim of injustice, he singled out Steve Haymes as his merciless persecutor, claiming that the probation officer had lied and distorted evidence to keep him behind bars.

"I taught my children to believe in the basic fairness of our system of justice," wrote Robinson in his neatly-typed letter to the judge, from Moberly Correctional Center. "They know now that justice is just a word and that the concept of justice in America is something that can be manipulated and used as a weapon by those empowered to enforce the law."

Complaining that the Clay County Court had dismissed his request for release and refused to modify his sentence, Robinson told the judge that he was an innocent man caught in a web of legal deceit and righteously demanded justice.

Although I have come to expect negative replies from the judicial and penal systems, I did hold a muted hope for some type of relief. Instead what I got was a double whammy. I guess we all underestimated the power of Mr. Haymes from the probation and parole department and his ability to keep me incarcerated. Since 1986, this man has done everything within his power to keep me in prison and to assure that the hand fell heavy on me and my family.

He has testified to falsehoods under oath, filed

false affidavits with the Missouri Court of Appeals, provided false and misleading information to the Kansas Department of Probation and Parole and now, once again has repeated his actions with the Missouri Parole Board where he has power because of his position.

Through Bruce [Houdek] we fought the false information he presented in court in 1986 and the false affidavit he presented to the Missouri Court of Appeals. Fortunately, that court saw through the smoke screen and sought the truth. They would not allow the blatant violation of my rights that he attempted. In their ruling dated July 19, 1996, they stated: "There cannot be the least doubt that the actions of the probation officer denied practitioner due process of law."

Robinson then went on to complain about Haymes "providing the same false and misleading information" to the Kansas Department of Probation and Parole. He claimed that, in November 1990, after great effort on his part, the court determined that the Parole Department's investigation was infected with false information.

Robinson continued:

"On April 17, 1991, my wife Nancy at my side, we appeared before a Parole Panel here at the Moberly Correctional Center. To our surprise and horror, the hearing officer began reciting the same false, erroneous and misleading information that I have fought now for six (6) years. She quoted from a newspaper article as if it were fact and had no record of the two (2) court rulings on the erroneous information."

Robinson then accused the Parole Panel of ignoring his many letters of recommendation and support, the reports from doctors and therapists, and the fact that restitution was made.

"In short," he wrote, they totally disregarded all the positive information and dealt only with information supplied by their employee. Their decision, "Becuase [sic] of the seriousness of the crime, I have been passed for release until the mandatory conditional release date June 16, 1994."

Robinson then began his plea to the judge:

"I understand that you withdrew from my case because of ethical considerations and that is why you personally could not consider my request for release. While I respect that, I wonder where are the ethics of those who continue to make sure I am confronted with false information and that that information is used to determine my freedom. . . .

"I am not asking for you to release me as I know that would be an improper request which the court could not consider. What I am asking is that the court enter an order to the Missouri Department of Corrections and the Missouri Parole Board to remove all the false and misleading information from my file, condider [sic] the information available from the Kansas Department of Corrections and all medical recommendations. Unless I can obtain an order from the court that directs the Board of Probation and Parole to use only factual information, I will never have an opportunity for a fair hearing. Since two courts have already ruled on this issue, the problem seems simple and should not pose any ethical questions.

Without such an order, I will remain in prison. If lucky, I will live long enough to get out but there will be little left. My ilnesses [sic] are degenerative and without proper rehabilitation, testing and long term treatment will continue to get worse. My physical impairments and right sided paralysis will not get better. Bruce [Houdek], my family and I all realize that the decisions made by the Clay County Court and the Missouri Parole Board amount to a sentence of death. Our only question, is this what is considered proportionate punishment for my crime in Missouri?

The letter, which was copied to his wife Nancy and attorney Bruce Houdek, did not sway Judge Mahoney or the Clay County Court in the slightest. A few days later Clay County Circuit Clerk Rita Fuller wrote Houdek:

The Court has reviewed this matter to determine if, pursuant to statute, it would be appropriate to recall the defendant from the Dept. of Corrections for the purpose of placing defendant on probation. Having considered the matter the court determines it would be inappropriate in this cause and declines to do so.

But as always, John Robinson relentlessly pressed on with his campaign for freedom, using his charm and intelligence to manipulate the doctors and jail staff he had managed to win over to his side. He was so successful that he even caused divisiveness among the prison doctors and the Probation Board.

On May 22, 1991, after being briefed by the sympathetic Dr. King, the Missouri Department of Corrections' Chief of Professional Services, Robert Schoenen, personally wrote to the Board of Probation and Parole, saying Robinson's life was at risk if he remained in jail.

Describing him as "a 47-year-old white male who has extensive, serious medical ailments," Schoenen wrote that Robinson had "experienced a severe heart attack" in 1987 and now suffered "severe chest pains with minimal exertion."

That June and July, John Robinson was brought to the prison infirmary on four separate occasions, after complaining of chest pains. Each time he displayed stroke-like symptoms and his doctors increased his medication, placing him on beta-blockers to control his angina.

Three months later Dr. King wrote to Schoenen, demanding to know why no official action had been taken to free Robinson.

"I have difficulty understanding why our earlier joint recommendation was not followed. I must assume that the parole board is not completely aware of the serious nature of this inmate's illnesses, or they are relying on the opinions of non-medical personnel in making their decisions."

CHAPTER 12

BEVERLY BONNER

AT the beginning of 1992, Inmate John Robinson was transferred to the Western Missouri Correctional Center in Cameron, to complete his sentence. Situated off US Highway 69, forty miles to the north of Kansas City, it was far nearer for Nancy Robinson and her children, who were regular visitors.

Opened just two years earlier, the main prison complex is laid out within a large octagon. It is a medium security facility that houses 2,619 prisoners, mainly serving sentences for drugs and alcohol-related offenses. It was also far more relaxed than Hutchinson or Moberly, accepting prisoners from other states under a cell-leasing program to finance construction costs.

The correctional center's genial physician, Dr. William Bonner, soon got to know John Robinson, who became a regular visitor to his busy practice. But unlike the prison doctors at Moberly, Dr. Bonner did not consider him a very sick man and certainly not on his deathbed.

"I treated him because he'd had a stroke," said Dr. Bonner. "I thought he was more in recovery from his prior illnesses."

Dr. Bonner, who was on good terms with most of the prisoners, remembers Robinson as a "businessman-type con artist," who was "well-spoken grammatically" and far more intelligent than the standard inmate.

"He was easy to talk to and more personable but there were so many inmates that went through my office during the five years I was there. He didn't stand out or make a big impression."

About eighteen months after John Robinson arrived, Dr. Bonner's wife Beverly was appointed prison librarian. She was amazed to discover that her new library assistant was none other than John Robinson, whom she'd met twenty years earlier, when they'd both worked at the Kansas City offices of Mobil Oil.

Brought up in a middle-class family on Long Island, Beverly had moved to Kansas City to study at the University of Missouri, where she got a degree in journalism. Later she passed certificates in teaching and librarianship.

After finishing her studies, she stayed on and married Joseph Lake, finding an executive position at Mobil Oil on West 10th Street in Kansas City. She was a workaholic, juggling her job as a division supervisor with bringing up her two small sons, Ryan and Randall.

As she and John Robinson worked in different departments, it is impossible to know how much contact they had there. But she must have been aware of his 1970 firing, as it was the subject of much company gossip.

Jim Chappell, who worked with Beverly at Mobil, remembers her as "a sharp gal," who was very hardworking and extremely "businesslike."

Beverly remained at Mobil until 1981, when she divorced Joseph Lake, keeping custody of her two sons. In 1987 a friend introduced her to Dr. William Bonner and they soon married, settling down in Cameron, Missouri, where he worked as the prison physician.

"She was an attractive person," says Dr. Bonner. "She was very outgoing and ambitious and always active in church functions and social activities."

Beverly felt that her new assistant was a kindred spirit, and she and John Robinson spent long hours reorganizing the library and updating its outmoded computer system. And then police say, they started a passionate love affair behind bars.

"I had no knowledge of what went on in the library since the medical department was quite a distance from there," explained Dr. Bonner, who later began to suspect something was amiss.

Over the six months they worked in the prison library, the middle-aged Bonner apparently confided that she was bored in her marriage and craved a more challenging job. Robinson told her of his ambitious plans to resurrect his Hydro-Gro company when he was released. He forecast that it would make a killing, as people in the nineties were far more attuned to organic vegetables than they had been ten years earlier.

Robinson's big talk certainly impressed Bonner, who was evidently flattered when he invited her to help him run the company after he got out of jail. He told her it would entail much foreign travel, something she had always dreamed of.

As they started planning their new life on his release, the fact that he was still married to Nancy and had four children did not seem to enter the equation. She believed him when he told her he was an innocent man, railroaded into jail by unscrupulous probation officials. One night she even discussed Robinson with her husband over dinner. Dr. Bonner, who only knew him as a patient, had no idea of the affair.

Around this time Beverly became good friends with an elderly lady named Eugenia Reece. The two had met when Eugenia, then in her mid-seventies, had arrived at Beverly's front door one night, selling Avon products.

Eugenia started baby-sitting Ryan and Randy regularly. "She had two of the cutest little boys and I love children," said Eugenia. "We became very good friends."

Overnight Beverly confided that she would soon leave her husband and start a "new line of work" in Kansas City.

"She never mentioned John Robinson by name but she was so thrilled that she would be going overseas," said Eugenia.

In the spring of 1993, John Robinson, now forty-nine years old, was finally released from the Western Missouri Correctional Center on probation. He had served almost six years behind bars in Kansas and Missouri.

Nancy Robinson was managing the Southfork Mobile Home Community in Belton, Missouri, and he moved into her trailer at 464 Valeen Lane. It was a long way from the affluence of Pleasant Valley. The Robinsons decided to leave Kansas City and relocate to Big Key in South Florida, where the dollar went further.

Robinson started contacting Florida realtors but did not have enough money to buy property. But he told them to keep him apprised of anything new coming onto the market, saying he would be able to afford a place next year.

Soon after Robinson's release Dr. Bonner found out about his wife's extra-marital affair. They agreed to divorce and her two sons from her first marriage went to live with their father in Kansas City North, as she prepared to move out of their home.

"I suspected she was having an affair with someone but I had no idea who," Dr. Bonner said.

Their divorce was finalized in February 1994 at a court hearing, with the doctor agreeing to pay Beverly eighteen thousand dollars as part of a property settlement. That would be the last time he would ever see Beverly alive.

*   *   *

A few weeks after her divorce, Beverly Bonner, now forty-nine, moved to Olathe to be near John Robinson and help him run the latest incarnation of Hydro-Gro. After an emotional farewell, she gave Eugenia Reece some of her potted plants to care for, and promised to keep in touch. Bonner asked Eugenia to pick up her mail and the magazines she subscribed to, and send them to a post office box at the Mail Room in the Crossroads Shopping Center in Olathe, which she would be using as a forwarding address. The post office box had recently been opened by John Robinson, using the alias "James Turner," and it was the same one where she had told her ex-husband to send her monthly thousand-dollar checks from their divorce settlement.

Soon after she arrived in Olathe, Beverly called her mother to say everything was going well. She spoke enthusiastically about her new job with John Robinson, whom she had mentioned in a previous conversation. Now, inexplicably, she announced that she was soon going overseas to work in the perfume industry.

A few days later she called back, sounding very upset. She told her mother that she had been mistaken in calling her new boss John Robinson, as it was not his real name. She insisted her mother erase the name "John Robinson" in her address book and replace it with "John Redmond."

When the company was officially incorporated in Missouri in late 1993, Beverly Bonner was listed as company president and registered agent, as Robinson was a convicted felon. Its company address was given as 1047 E. Blue Ridge Boulevard, Kansas City, Missouri. Nowhere in the Missouri articles of incorporation is John Robinson even mentioned, although there is a "James Turner" listed as company secretary.

A few months before her husband's release, Nancy

Robinson had rented out two storage units at Stor-Mor For Less on Highway 58 in Raymore, Missouri taking one in each of their names.

Then in November 1993, John Robinson arrived one morning to take a third larger unit. He gave the manager Delores Fields (not her real name) a deposit, saying he would come in and pay monthly.

"He said he wanted the unit for his sister Beverly," said Fields. "She was going off to Australia to work for his Hydro-Gro company and it was for her house storage."

On a freezing morning that winter, Robinson arrived at Stor-Mor For Less, driving Beverly Bonner's van. He pulled up outside his new unit and began unloading a large sealed metal barrel, which he carefully placed inside with the rest of her possessions.

On his way out of the gate, Fields asked him how his sister was doing and Robinson replied that she was now in Italy.

"Oh she's having a ball," he said. "I don't think she'll be coming back."

Soon after Beverly Bonner told her family and friends she was going abroad, they began receiving one-page typewritten letters from all over the world, saying she was having a great time. Her ex-husband, Dr. Bonner, who had no idea Beverly had taken a job with Robinson, got one from Scandinavia and never questioned its authenticity, as it appeared to be signed by his ex-wife.

"I was not suspicious," he remembers. "It was just about general things. She asked how the boys were doing and spoke about all the interesting places she was seeing. It was just something somebody would write on a postcard."

Eugenia Reece also received letters bearing her

John Robinson, seen here at far left, in full scouting uniform in the early 30s. (Courtesy of Scott Davis)

John:

I am really sorry about this but you have just been fucked out of your money! I also took your car, I will write and let either you or that dumb shit Ralph know were I leave the car. I would imagine that Larry is really going to be pissed at you, I -ot you money, your car, Ralphs money and Larry shit. Not a bad haul in one day.

Tell Ralphie that it serves him right for treating me soooooo bad! I gave him everything and got nothing back in return from him.

I don't know what he wants. His kid was over the other day at his place and he doesn't even want to stay.

I hope you understand. I didn't want to screw you up and I know Larry is going to be looking for me, but by the time you read this I will be long gone.

If you go to the cops about your car, I will have to tell them all about your dealings and Raphs too. So jsut both of you be cool, I will make sure you know how to get your car back. I haven't decided on cleveland, chicago o denver, oh well.

Love ya,

Paula

The letter that Paula Godfrey allegedly wrote to Robinson. Authoritie
believe Robinson wrote the letter and forged Paula's name.
(Courtesy of Bill Godfrey)

The Robinsons' house in an affluent suburb of Kansas City, where the family lived prior to Robinson's arrest in 1989. (John Glatt)

The Robinsons' trailer home at Santa Barbara Estates, from which John Robinson prowled the Internet. (John Glatt)

The bedroom at the Extended StayAmerica Hotel where several of victims stayed. (John Glatt)

Beverly Bonner, the prison librarian whose body was later discovered along with those of Sheila and Debbie Faith. (Courtesy of Dr. William Bonner)

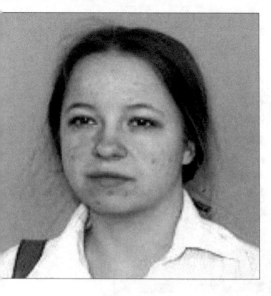

Izabella
Lewicka.
(Courtesy of
Dustin Sims)

Suzette
Trouten.
(Courtesy of
Kim Padilla)

Cass County District Attorney Chris Koster, who is prosecuting Robinson on behalf of the state of Missouri.
(Photo compliments of *The Cass County Democrat Missourian*)

Johnson County District Attorney Paul Morrison. Chris Koster stands a left. (Photo compliments of *The Cass County Democrat Missourian*)

e lock to John Robinson's storage locker, where the bodies of three mur-
red women were found. The "SM", presumably short for Slavemaster,
n clearly be seen. (John Glatt)

uzette Trouten, seen here on the left, poses with Crystal Ferguson.
ourtesy of Crystal Ferguson)

The Johnson County Court House, where John Robinson will be tried, America's first alleged Internet serial killer. (John Glatt)

The complete case file against John Robinson at the Lenexa Police Department. (John Glatt)

friend's signature over the next two years. So did Beverly's mother, who received a letter postmarked from Amsterdam—a city John Robinson was well acquainted with from his 1980s vacation. It even accurately described a Dutch street which Beverly's mother had once visited. The last letter arrived in January 1997, with a Russian postmark on the envelope. It said that Beverly was on her way to Amsterdam and then off on a new assignment to China, ending: "Remember that I love you, and I'll be in touch."

From all the letters, her mother got the impression that Beverly worked for a company that was headquartered in the Netherlands. Employees would go off on long trips and then return to Amsterdam to receive their next assignment.

In December 1995 Beverly's eldest son Randy died and she was the only member of the family who didn't attend the funeral.

"I thought that was strange," said her ex-husband, who has now left the prison service, remarried and runs a family practice in Stockton, Missouri. "I thought she was in Europe at that time and couldn't come back."

He figured she must be all right as each month like clockwork his bank would send back his cancelled thousand-dollar checks, after they had been cashed.

CHAPTER 13

PREYING INTO CYBERSPACE

WHILE John Robinson was in jail, computers had taken a quantum leap forward, and on his release he was well prepared to take full advantage. Ironically, Hutchinson Prison had given him a computing master class and he now extended his activities out into cyberspace. There he could remain faceless, while preying on the countless vulnerable women out there. Now he had now found his true instrument of torture and would play it like a virtuoso.

First developed in the early 1960s by the Department of Defense to allow scientific researchers to exchange information, the Internet soon became an essential communication tool. By the mid-1990s the Internet was up and running for the masses, linking millions of people all over the world and providing unlimited opportunities for an unscrupulous confidence trickster.

He would also be able to operate his criminal enterprises from home, under a cloak of anonymity. And be able to communicate with his colleagues in the International Council of Masters, using BDSM chat rooms to recruit new slaves for its meetings.

One of the first things he did as a free man was buy a couple of desktop computers and sign up with an Internet service provider to gain access. Allegedly dubbing himself "The Slavemaster," he now began to trawl the net, searching for victims in bondage and sadomasochistic chat rooms and personal ads. He carefully cultivated his Internet persona, portraying himself as a successful, middle-aged businessman with a farm and horses, well experienced in the BDSM lifestyle.

He cunningly related to the women he met online, prying out their weaknesses and then offering to fulfill their dreams. It was not too far removed from the deceptive methods he had employed for years, but by harnessing the Internet he would chillingly take his activities into the twenty-first century.

Sheila Dale Faith came from a broken home and would spend her life searching for love and security. Born Sheila Howell in 1948 in Dallas, Texas, her parents divorced when she was five years old. Then her mother took her and her brothers and sisters to live with their grandmother.

Soon afterwards her mother walked out on the family, leaving their elderly grandmother to bring up all five children alone. Later, when Sheila's mother had a change of heart and returned for them, the grandmother refused to give them back.

Sheila grew up an overweight and needy child. She was a very lonely teenager, often teased at school about her plain looks. But everything changed when she met John Faith in the late 1970s and they married in Dallas.

In 1979 they had a baby girl they named Debbie, who was diagnosed with cerebral palsy. Bringing up their handicapped child was a constant struggle for the Faiths, who had little money and often relied on food stamps to survive. In the mid-1980s the family moved to the less expensive Fullerton, California, and found a cheaper apartment within driving distance of the beach.

Debbie, who was confined to a wheelchair and wore braces on both arms, was sent to Nicholas Junior High School, where her pleasant, outgoing personality won her many close friends. She loved challenging the other pupils to wheelchair races and was passionate about watching the daytime soap operas.

But everything changed when John Faith died of cancer in summer 1991 and Sheila and Debbie's world fell apart. They buried his ashes under the pier at Huntington Beach, where they had enjoyed some of their happiest times, then went back to their apartment to grieve.

Sheila was now forced to go on welfare, receiving just $1,016 a month from Social Security to feed and clothe herself and her disabled teenage daughter. Debbie, at thirteen, weighed over two hundred pounds and her mother, who was hugely overweight herself, had to use a hoist to get her daughter into bed at night.

As Debbie's condition worsened, she had just enough movement in one of her hands to control the buttons on her electric wheelchair. But the unfortunate young girl tried to live as normal a life as possible, never dwelling on her medical problems. She inspired her friends with her optimism and vowed against all medical opinion that one day she would get out of her wheelchair and walk.

Since her husband's death, Sheila had become increasingly lonely and was desperate to find a new romance. She dreamed of a wealthy white knight who would rescue her and her daughter from a miserable life of poverty. She also became obsessed with pornographic pictures, which she put up on her bedroom wall.

As an escape, she began answering lonely hearts ads in newspapers and using her daughter's new computer to search for suitable men in online chat rooms. Soon she announced that they were moving to Santa Cruz in Northern California, where she had found two prospective boyfriends—the fact that they were married did not seem to matter. Debbie did not want to leave her friends behind, but the good-natured girl knew how lonely her mother was and wanted her to be happy.

They arrived in Santa Cruz in 1993 and found an apartment, where Sheila started inviting one of the men over once or twice a week for sex. Before he arrived she would give Debbie and her new best friend Suzanne Lawrence, who was also disabled, spending money to stay out of the house so they could be alone.

One day a frightened Debbie Faith told her friend that the man had been sexually suggestive to her, and she did not know what to do. When Suzanne's mother, Debbie Lawrence, heard, she said she wasn't worried as Sheila was an "excellent mother" and could be "trusted." Later, to their horror, they read in the paper that the man was under investigation for molesting little girls. As for Sheila's other Santa Cruz boyfriend, he was "crazy" and a "loser," Debbie Faith told her friend.

Then Sheila found new romance on the Internet and told her daughter that they were moving again. This time they were going 1,250 miles east to Colorado, so she could be with him. Coincidentally, their long-time Orange County friends, Manuel and Nancy Guerrero, had just relocated to Pueblo, Colorado, and offered to help them move and find accommodation. Manuel flew to Santa Cruz and drove the Faiths and all their worldly possessions back to Pueblo in Sheila's battered old white 1978 Chevrolet van, which broke down three times during the journey.

But Sheila Faith's new romance was short-lived and in January 1994, she told Debbie they would be moving east to Kansas City. This time, she assured her daughter, she had really found the man of her dreams.

John Robinson, police say, had spent weeks wooing Sheila Faith, first in an Internet chat room and then over the telephone. It wouldn't have taken him long to get

her to open up and tell him all about her sad, lonely life
and she soon fell in love with him.

Sheila was most impressed when he told her he was
a wealthy Kansas City businessman and owned a large
farm and horses. She never thought it strange when he
closely questioned her about their monthly Social Security payments, asking for names and addresses of family and close friends.

Blinded by happiness, Sheila, who now weighed over
200 pounds, was delighted when "John" invited her and
her daughter to come and live in Kansas City. He promised to find her a good job and even suggested a special
school he knew of for Debbie, who would be able to
have her friends come to stay, and learn to ride his
horses.

Nancy Guerrero was shocked when Sheila announced
one day that she had met her "dream man," and was
moving across the country to Kansas to live on his farm.
Highly skeptical, she warned her friend that it all
sounded too good to be true. But Sheila refused to listen,
saying "John" was the nicest man she had ever met and
they had a future together.

Late one summer's night in 1994, John Robinson arrived at the Faiths' front door to drive them to Kansas.
There was much excitement as he helped load their suit-
cases and Debbie's wheelchair into the back of the white
Chevrolet van. Then, police say, he drove them off into
the night and they were never seen alive again.

Nancy Guerrero arrived at the Faiths' house the day after
they left, and was shocked to find them gone. When she
had last seen Sheila the night before, she had never once
mentioned that they were leaving so soon. The Faiths
had also not told their landlord, Art Cordova, that they
were moving out. When he went in to inspect the house

he found all their furniture and most of their belongings still there.

Soon after they disappeared, Sheila Faith's younger brother, William Howell, like other family members, began receiving typed letters with her signature, assuring him that they were all right and happy in their new life. When he became suspicious and called the Social Security Administration to find out where Sheila and Debbie's welfare checks were going, he was told it was private, restricted information that not even close family members could be given.

In the fall of 1994, the Social Security Administration received a medical report purportedly signed by Beverly Bonner's husband, Dr. William R. Bonner, stating that Debbie Faith was now "totally disabled" and would need "complete care for the rest of her life."

The letter also instructed the government department to forward all the Faiths' future welfare checks to "James Turner's" post office box at the Mail Room in Olathe. It was the same one where Beverly Bonner's checks and magazines were being sent.

Two days after Christmas in 1995, John Robinson celebrated his fifty-second birthday with his family at their trailer home in Valeen Lane. Among the guests were their youngest daughter Christy and her fiancé, Kyle Shipps, an ambitious young police officer with the Prairie Village Police Department. Ironically, Officer Shipps—who married Christy on January 6, 1996—had recently rubbed shoulders with one of Kansas City's most notorious murderesses.

Three months earlier, Officer Shipps, who is now a detective for the same police department, had played a minor role in the infamous Dr. Debora Green murder case. Dr. Green would later admit to trying to poison her husband, and to setting her mansion on fire, killing two of her three young children.

Just prior to the murders, Officer Shipps and his Sergeant, Wes Jordan, had been summoned on a "mental" call by a dispatcher to the house of Dr. Michael Farrar. The wealthy Prairie Village doctor wanted to get his wife Debora committed to an institution as he considered her dangerously unstable.

Debora Green had been drinking heavily all day and by the evening was threatening suicide. When Officer Shipps and Sergeant Jordan arrived at their luxury mansion in Canterbury Court, Prairie Village, they were met by Dr. Farrar, who led them into the house, where they walked past two little girls and a boy huddled together in the entrance.

Officer Shipps then went up to Debora Green's bedroom at the rear of the house and found her half-naked on the bed, obviously very drunk. For the next forty-five minutes Shipps talked to Dr. Green and tried to calm her down, as she continuously banged her head against the wall. Then he drove her to the Kansas University Medical Center, where she had once practiced medicine.

A month later Dr. Green would deliberately burn down their mansion, killing her children, Tim and Kelly Farrar, in a demented attempt to win back her husband's affections. At a later preliminary hearing, Officer Shipps would be questioned by Johnson County Prosecutor Paul Morrison about the dreadful night he spent with Dr. Green.

The Debora Green case was a huge news story in Kansas City and was closely followed by Officer Shipps' future father-in-law, John Robinson.

Since leaving the penitentiary, John Robinson had been careful to keep a low profile and attend regular meetings with his probation officer. To his relief the police and FBI investigations had been wound up when he'd gone to jail in 1987. Still missing, Paula Godfrey, Lisa and Tiffany Stasi and Catherine Clampitt had been forgotten, except by their families.

Once a month, according to eyewitnesses, Robinson would drive to the Mail Room on Santa Fe Street in Olathe to pick up the checks for Beverly Bonner and the Faiths. And by December 1995, he apparently had enough money for him and Nancy to put down $95,000 for a two-bedroom ranch-style house, and an empty lot next door, on Big Pine Key, Florida. It would be a present for their eldest son John Jr. and his wife Lisa, who had just made them grandparents.

After finalizing the deal on the Big Key property, John Robinson and his favorite son drove to Florida to clear the lot and build a playground. Robinson had previously written to the real estate broker, handling the property at 31040 Avenue F in the Key's Sands District, saying that he would make a walk-through inspection. He requested that the key be given to John Jr., who would be taking care of the house until he and Nancy could move in.

Father and son spent about a month working at the property, which John Jr. and his wife would later turn into a kindergarten, called Kids Key Daycare Inc. The plan was for his son's family to move into the two-bedroom house. Then Robinson would build a new house on the adjoining vacant lot for him and Nancy.

But he soon ran into problems when he discovered it would be impossible to build on the lot, as there was a sinkhole and abandoned septic tanks. He then fired off a furious letter to his realtor, who had handled the deal, threatening to sue if she didn't pay him the several thousand dollars for the necessary repairs. Later he had his new Kansas City attorney write the realtor, asking for the five thousand dollars that Robinson claimed to have spent on structural repairs to the property. He also demanded a further twelve thousand dollars for removing septic tanks, obtaining a warranty on the house and attorney fees.

The realtor then threatened to tell Robinson's mortgage lender that he had lied on his loan application, claiming that he would be residing at the house and not his son. Robinson finally backed down, as he was still under probation, and John Jr.'s family moved to Big Key while he and Nancy remained in Kansas City.

CHAPTER 14

SLAVE CONTRACT

IN the wake of the Big Pine fiasco, Nancy Robinson got a new job managing the Santa Barbara Mobile Home Park in Olathe. It was a promotion over her last job and the Robinsons moved their mobile trailer home to a vacant lot at 36 Monterey Lane, a prime area at the back of the estate.

The always house-proud John Robinson began building an extension onto the side of his trailer, and landscaping the small back garden with a barbecue area. He also added some homely touches of his own, decorating his front patio with rows of potted pink geraniums, placing a religious statue in the center of a flowerbed and a Liberty Bell up front, next to a sign that read, "GRANDPA'S PLACE. WE SPOIL GRANDCHILDREN."

Nancy Robinson soon made her presence felt among the middle-class residents of Santa Barbara's 484 trailer homes. Since her husband had gone to jail, her personality had undergone a dramatic transformation. The six years she had lived alone appeared to have given her a new confidence. The once shy, reclusive wife whom everybody pitied, now seemed to dominate the relationship. The balance of power had shifted as she no longer expected him to remain faithful and they now had an unspoken understanding, where they led completely separate lives.

"Nancy was very strict," said Santa Barbara resident Layne Hudson. "She didn't make any bones about yelling at people who lived here. If someone was driving

too fast down the road she would yell at them to slow
down."

Some residents even felt sorry for "mild-mannered"
John Robinson, feeling that his wife dominated him.
Others complained that he was a "dirty old man," who
propositioned female residents for sex. Late at night
Robinson would often prowl around the spacious estate
in a golf-cart, acting suspiciously.

"He knew our schedule," said Hudson. "He drove past
my house a lot when my husband was away nights working and I was by myself. If my husband was home he'd
only drive by once. It made me uncomfortable."

He came on even stronger to Joy Friedman, a married
mother living on the same street as the Robinsons. He
would arrive at her trailer and try to coax her into sex,
staring her in the eyes and saying, "Today?" When
Friedman threatened to tell Nancy, Robinson shrugged
it off, saying, "She don't care." But he never came
around again.

In April 1997, a few months after completing his
Kansas probation, John Robinson incorporated a new
company called Specialty Publications of America, in
Missouri. This time there was no smart office suite and
he converted a small bedroom at the front of his trailer
to use as his business base, setting up three sophisticated
computer systems, which were connected to each other.
Every day he worked long hours on his computers with
the shades drawn, often continuing late into the night.

"He told me he worked through the Internet," said
Sara Khan, a young mother, whose trailer was next door
to the Robinsons. "He was always on his computer and
said he was running a business, writing a newspaper for
mobile home parks."

Robinson's new free magazine, *Manufactured Modular Living*, soon ran into trouble, accused by rival local

trade publisher John Woolcroft of plagiarizing his long-established mobile home publication. When Woolcroft sent him a letter telling him to cease publication, Robinson just ignored him.

"It just looked like he lifted everything from my magazine," Woolcroft later told *The Kansas City Star*.

Over the next couple of years, Robinson became a controversial figure in the local mobile home trade community, as he regularly visited the area's trailer parks and shopping malls, selling advertising space. He even fostered a smart, new preppy image, complete with golf shirts, khaki shorts and loafers.

"That man was a constant black eye to us in the industry," remembers Tom Hagar, president of Mid-America Home Center Inc. "His articles would give suggestions to home owners that ran against all the standards in the industry. He didn't care."

Whenever he was challenged on the contents of his publication by someone in the trade, he would become abusive, angrily citing the First Amendment. But like his old Equi-II company, Robinson was using his new publishing venture to funnel cash from far more sinister enterprises that he was now involved in.

And as "The Slavemaster" he had allegedly begun a maze of relationships with women he had met online, who shared his fascination with BDSM.

Soon after moving to Santa Barbara, he met Lois Barlow (not her real name) in a chat room. The Tennessee woman, who was new to the BDSM lifestyle, was searching for a new master in the chat room one night when she encountered "The Slavemaster" and fell under his spell.

According to Barlow, Robinson offered to become her master if she signed a "slave contract," granting him absolute control over her body, mind and finances. She

agreed and he sent her the contract which she duly
signed and returned.

John Robinson's slave contract—which countless
women would sign over the next few years—had no
legal validity, although many of his slaves did not realize
this. Years later it would appear on "The Slavemaster" 's
own International Council of Masters Website, as a boil-
erplate guide to other masters.

SLAVE CONTRACT
**This is a basic contract that may be used
between a Master and slave**

Of my own free will, as of this day [date], I [name
of slave] (hereinafter called "SLAVE"), hereby grant
[Name of Master] (hereinafter called "MASTER"),
full ownership and use of my body and mind from
now until I am released.

I will place my sobriety/emotional sobriety first in all
considerations in this relationship.

I will obey my MASTER at all times and will whole-
heartedly seek your pleasure and well-being above all
other considerations. I renounce all my rights to my
own pleasure, comfort, or gratification except insofar
as you desire or permit them.

I will strive diligently to re-mold my body, my habits,
and my attitudes in accordance with your desires. I
will seek always to please you better, and will gracefully accept criticism as a means for growth and not
a threat of abandonment.

I renounce all rights to privacy or concealment from
you. . . .

I understand and agree that any failure by me to comply fully with your desires shall be regarded as sufficient cause for possibly severe punishment.

I understand that for a training period indicated by you all punishment will be given at a 5 to 1 ratio to the offense.

Within the limits of my physical safety and my ability to earn a livelihood, I otherwise unconditionally accept as your prerogative anything that you may choose to do with me, whether as punishment, for your amusement, or for whatever purpose, no matter how painful or humiliating to myself.

The contract then provides a space for the slave to identify a "safeword" to be used to indicate that things had gone too far, to communicate physical distress, "emotionally unsafe areas," or to bring the session to an end. There is also a space for the master's safeword, which he can use to end a "scene or activity."

In the next part of the contract, the slave promises to complete any assignment for the master within 48 hours, and to respond to all the master's communications within 24 hours. Then comes a section on "punishments":

I understand that if I use certain words which are deemed by you to be inappropriate for a SLAVE, the punishment will be automatic and then it is my duty to remind MASTER in the case that he fails to remember.

Finally, the contract sets forth a series of agreements:

I understand that at all times I am to be honest with
you and communicate my feelings (even if I
perceive that you may not approve). I understand
that no feeling I have can be wrong, and that
they may indicate a situation which needs
to be addressed.

Within the limits of my physical safety and my
ability to earn a livelihood, I otherwise
unconditionally accept as your prerogative anything
that you may choose to do with me, whether as
punishment, for your amusement,
or for whatever purpose.

I understand that my MASTER has my ultimate
physical, mental and spiritual well being in mind
and will strive to be worthy of his pride in all my
endeavors. I will at all times maintain a safe, sane
and consensual relationship.

Over the course of their five-year master/slave relationship, Barlow sent Robinson at least seventeen thousand dollars, including a check made payable to his
Specialty Publications company. She says she even
turned over her Individual Retirement Account for him
to invest. Later, when she asked him to account for the
money, he refused.

At one point he asked her to move to Kansas, offering
her a high-paying job working on computers for his
magazine. But she refused. Eventually, when the Internal
Revenue Service taxed her for cashing out her IRA, she
cancelled her slave contract, hiring a lawyer to get her
money back from Robinson.

"In a dominant/submissive relationship, someone who
is a con man has a very, very willing subject," said the

lawyer, who held little hope of Robinson ever repaying the money.

Marianne Castle (not her real name), a Washington DC–based writer who is in the BDSM lifestyle and a leading member of Black Rose, an organization that advises people on S&M safety, said that slave contracts were often signed by inexperienced dabblers online.

"It's a fantasy, a game," she explained. "You're going to be the slave and do everything for your master and give him all your money. If you are only experienced with BDSM online, you are more likely to sign something that's a lot of crap. In our society you cannot really be a slave."

In October 1998, Cindy Owens (not her real name), a nurse from Canada, placed a personal ad for a Master on a BDSM Website. Two weeks later she received a reply from a man calling himself "JR." He described himself as a divorced entrepreneur who owned five businesses and lived on his farm with horses.

After sending her two pictures of himself, JR asked her to supply intimate details of her sex life and erotic desires so he could decide if he wanted her as a slave. The forty-three-year-old woman complied and soon received his slave contract via e-mail, which she duly signed and returned.

Over the course of their six-month relationship in cyberspace, JR dispensed a daily schedule of explicit sexual tasks that she was expected to perform. They involved painful sexual toys that were to be attached to her nipples and genitalia, shaving off her pubic hair and the use of ice picks. He even wanted to brand her, burning his initials into her hip, which she agreed to let him do if they ever met.

"He made sure that I knew my body was his," said Owens. "That's part of being a slave."

Owens willingly complied with everything JR demanded she do. He made her ask his permission to attend BDSM meetings and no one was ever allowed to physically touch her body. And when she mentioned that she was searching for a new job in the United States, he offered her a supervisor's position in his non-existent hydroponic greenhouse. She was very tempted by his proposition and seriously considered it.

"I can't believe how close I came to moving down there," said Owens.

But something made her stall for time, after he asked her to meet him in Chicago for a BDSM session. JR grew impatient that she was taking too long to decide and the relationship cooled when he lost interest. But there were many other Internet slaves only too willing to come to Kansas and be brutalized by The Slavemaster.

CHAPTER 15

IZABELA LEWICKA

WHEN nineteen-year-old art student Izabela Lewicka encountered John Robinson in 1997 on the Internet, it was she who made the running. The attractive, red-haired teenager thought she had found the perfect Master, who would guide her through the BDSM lifestyle. And then she decided to surprise her new mentor, who was almost three times her age, by moving to Kansas to be near him.

Born in Poland in 1978, Izabela, and her younger sister, grew up under the repressive Communist regime where her father, Andrzei and mother Danuta, both worked as scientists. On November 25, 1993, after being granted permanent resident visas, the Lewickas emigrated to America, settling down in West Lafayette, Indiana.

The Lewickas soon adapted to American life and the family thrived. Andrzei found a job as physics lab coordinator at Purdue University, where Danuta got a position as an assistant research scientist.

Izabela, who was then fifteen, hardly spoke any English and took lessons with a neighbor, Margaret Mannering, before enrolling in Harrison High School. She joined the high school color guard and practiced her flag routines in her garden, to the amusement of neighbors. But soon she dropped out of the color guard and started rebelling against conformity.

Izabela had always been a talented artist and now she decided to become a fashion designer, wearing long, brightly-colored Victorian dresses with free-flowing skirts, ankle bracelets and sandals. She also got her nose pierced and hung out with fringe groups at school.

As a high school upperclassman, she passionately threw herself into pottery, photography and painting, taking extra courses at Purdue University. And she impressed many by spending months designing and painting an elaborate, giant mural on the wall of the University's Wesley Foundation. Wesley's associate campus minister, Pat Sleeth, remembers Lewicka as highly talented and unconventional.

"She was very open and friendly," says Sleeth. "She worked right near the front door [and] as people came in, she would make a point of greeting them even if she didn't know them."

At Harrison High, Izabela was a key member of the self-appointed intellectual set of students who gathered in coffee houses on the Purdue Campus, debating politics and the arts. But outside of the group she was "kinda shy, except with her friends," remembers her former classmate, Karl Van Zandt.

Another classmate, Kendra Montgomery, thought her art was "inspirational" and came straight from her soul.

"She was just really, so involved in art," said Montgomery. "That was really her contribution to our high school."

When Izabela graduated in 1996, her father took her to France on a tour of universities, as she wanted to study fashion design abroad. But she decided against it, enrolling instead in a fine arts program at Purdue University's School of Liberal Arts in August 1996.

Nine months later, after meeting John Robinson over the Internet, nineteen-year-old Izabela astonished everyone by dropping out of her studies and moving to Kansas City. Robinson would later tell one of his Internet slaves that Izabela had suddenly sent him an e-mail announcing that she was on her way to Kansas to be with him.

"He was embarrassed," said the slave who had placed a personal ad on a BDSM site, which was answered by Robinson and had led to a relationship. "He said he hadn't asked her to come there and she had taken off and left college to be with him."

Robinson told her that he had first seen Izabela in person in a Kansas City restaurant and was "embarrassed" by her all-black gothic clothes, black lipstick and piercings. According to Robinson, he initially told her to go back to Indiana, but she became very emotional. He finally relented when she begged him to stay, offering herself as his permanent sex slave.

Izabela found an apartment in Westport, the arty, bohemian section of Kansas City, and began working as a layout artist, handling the advertising for Robinson's mobile home trade magazines.

Soon after arriving, she enthusiastically wrote her parents letters of her travels to Europe and California. They had no idea their teenage daughter was embroiled in a torrid sado-masochistic affair with a man old enough to be her grandfather. Robinson in turn would tell friends that Izabela was the daughter of a business associate.

A few months after moving to Kansas, Lewicka, who had dyed her hair reddish brown, and Robinson went to the Johnson County Courthouse in Olathe to take out a marriage license. Robinson, who had been married to Nancy for thirty-two years, gave his name as "John Anthony Robinson" and his real birth date. Izabela entered hers as "Isabela Katyzma Lewicka," claiming that she had been born in the 1940s.

Although the couple apparently never collected their marriage license or went through a ceremony, Izabela added "Robinson" to her name, telling friends she was now a married woman.

In the fall of 1998, Robinson found her an apartment in Overland Park, so they would be closer to each other and she enrolled for a semester at the Johnson County Community College.

By early 1998, Lewicka was a frequent visitor to the Santa Barbara Estates, where she worked on Robinson's magazines. When freelance graphic artist Pamela Guthrie was hired by Robinson to design an issue of *Manufactured Modular Living*, Lewicka told her he was her uncle. But the couple's over-intimate behavior puzzled Guthrie.

"He'd have his hands all over her," said Guthrie. "Hands on her back, across her shoulder, resting near her breast. I thought, 'That's no uncle.' "

After two months working for Robinson, Guthrie resigned after he refused to pay the $1,800 he owed her.

In January 1999, Izabela Lewicka was driving home through Overland Park when she scratched a parked car belonging to Tony Hough. When he later called Lewicka, who had not reported the accident, John Robinson came on the phone and told Hough to deal with him directly, as Lewicka hardly spoke English.

"He was very obstinate, very difficult," said Hough, "at times rude, in fact."

When Hough reported the matter to the Overland Park Police Department, Robinson took a series of photographs of Lewicka's car to prove that her bumper could not have caused the scratches to Hough's blue car.

Overland Park Police Officer Daryl Hasenleder was sent to investigate, and became very suspicious after interviewing Robinson and Lewicka separately. Lewicka told Officer Hasenleder that she was Robinson's wife, giving her surname as "Robinson," while John Robinson maintained that she was merely his cousin.

"I asked Miss Robinson why John would lie?" said Hasenleder in his official report of the incident. "She said they didn't want anyone to know who they were or where they lived because people were rude to them."

She explained that she didn't live with Robinson at the Santa Barbara Estates as "It would not be proper."

Eventually, in March, Lewicka admitted the traffic charges and paid Hough $367.07 in restitution.

During the two-and-a-half years Izabela Lewicka lived in Overland Park, she became a regular customer at A. Friendley's Used and Rare Bookstore. Once a month she would scour the store looking for books on art, the occult, witchcraft and poisonous plants. The slightly overweight girl, who always dressed in black, made an impression on the store's owner, Robert Meyers, and his wife Diane.

"She was a very nice person and very friendly," remembers Robert Meyers. "She said she was from where the real Dracula was from in Europe and she bought fictional books on Vlad the Impaler and other works on the occult."

Izabela told Meyers that she was an avid reader of the occult and often left the store with a stack of books on the subject. Once she paid him $100 for a rare edition of *Patterns*, by her favorite horror writer, Pat Cadigan.

"She told me that her husband was much older," said Meyers. "That's all she ever said about him."

On July 18, 1999, Robinson came in the store with Lewicka, who announced that her "husband" would be buying her books today. Robinson looked uncomfortable, like he couldn't wait to leave the store, as he stood impatiently watching Izabela browse the occult bookshelves.

"My wife said he gave her the creeps and stared at her funny," said Meyers. "He wasn't a book lover, I could tell, and he didn't buy anything, although she did."

On their way out, she told the Meyerses that it would be her last visit as she was moving away. She did not elaborate further on where she might be going.

By the beginning of 1999, The Slavemaster was becoming well-known to the BDSM online community. He spent hours every day prowling S&M Websites and chat rooms, searching for lonely, subservient women.

No one will ever know for certain just how many women John Robinson met online, and investigators believe it could run into the hundreds. The community is highly secretive and many of its players are married professionals, who carefully mask their identities, afraid that exposure would jeopardize their jobs and personal lives, because of the stigma that surrounds bondage and domination.

Robinson knew only too well how vulnerable these women were, and cruelly exploited them.

"A lot of [women] have suppressed their fantasies for many, many years," said Marianne Castle of Blackrose. "Then, all of a sudden they realize they are not alone and are not such freaks after all. And then they're vulnerable."

In early 1999, Lauralei Meadows (not her real name), a 52-year-old Kentucky grandmother with a degree, who ran her own medical business, placed a personal ad on the contacts page of a bondage Website under the pseudonym "Heavensent." Describing herself as a "Submissive" in need of a "Dom/Master" for a long-term relationship and eventual real-life encounter, she desired specialized training in various aspects of bondage, which she practiced daily.

In her introduction she wrote: "I am a tall, slender, dark blonde professional lady who loves to serve a special Master! I am a very submissive type person as far as sex goes and anything but submissive in the other areas of my life! I love family, the outdoors, good friends and good sex! I have three grown children and one beautiful grandson! My favorite outdoor activity is anything to do with the lake or the ocean! Nascar racing as well as Univ. of Ky. Basketball and football are favorites also! I have had about 6 months r/l [real life] 24/7 live-in experience with a loving, strict Master and loved every minute of it! That relationship has now ended and I am looking for a new Master to serve!"

After stating up front that she had no interest in married men or anyone under the age of forty-five, Lauralei said she was looking for "a loving/strict Master" with the knowledge and resources to "train and take care of his personal property." She wanted someone "to train this true submissive to do things only he wishes."

A few days later she received an e-mail from "Jim Turner," saying that he was interested in becoming her Master. He told Lauralei he was a successful businessman, working in a social services department of a large corporation. He was divorced but still on good terms with his ex-wife, whom he lunched with once a month.

"He seemed like the perfect gentleman," she says. "I was looking for a financially secure man who wasn't into playing games, as I didn't want to support them."

Jim Turner e-mailed Lauralei two pictures of himself in full-denim Western attire, complete with a Stetson hat. In the pictures he has a warm smile and looks very laid-back, casually resting his foot on a tree stump in a field.

He suggested that they have a BDSM cyber-sex relationship, and when Lauralei told him her brother was

dying of cancer, Turner became very sympathetic, offering to do anything he could to help. Initially their
relationship involved some BDSM role play, but it soon
became mostly platonic, as they corresponded about
their families and everyday lives.

Believing it might develop into a serious relationship,
Lauralei pictured Jim Turner as a loving father and
clever businessman with a big heart. She also thought
he sounded "fascinating and interesting." When he invited her to come and visit him in Kansas she was
tempted, but told him they should first get to know each
other better online.

Lauralei and the "charming" Jim Turner exchanged
daily e-mails during the three months they corresponded. At one point she didn't hear from him for
three or four days, and when she asked him why, he
replied that he had been out of town as his daughter
was having a baby.

About a month into the relationship, Lauralei felt so
comfortable that she gave Turner her telephone number
and he called her several times. But she noticed that his
caller ID always came up "unavailable," and he always
made some excuse not to give her his phone number.

When her brother died, Lauralei was heartbroken and
e-mailed Turner the sad news.

"He sent me back an e-mail saying I should lean on
him and let him help me with my problems," she said.
"Then for some reason, and I've no idea why, I never
answered him and that was the last time we were in
touch."

In September 1999, John Robinson sold the property at
Big Pine Key and used the money to buy a piece of land
a few miles south of La Cygne, Kansas. The sixteen-
and-a-half acres of land in Linn County contained a cou-

ple of outbuildings and a pond and was valued at $36,670.

The ramshackle property, which Robinson proudly referred to as his "farm," lies a couple of miles north of a high school and is surrounded by farms growing corn and soybeans. Duck hunting is popular, and there are several clubs in the area. Soon after purchase Robinson bought an old trailer with a deck from the Santa Barbara Estates, that had recently been repossessed by a finance company, and had one of his wife's maintenance staff help him move it onto the farm.

The locals in La Cygne, which means "City of Swans" in French, seldom saw Robinson after he took over the property and began fencing it in. But it wasn't long before he was involved in a bitter lawsuit with his neighbors, Max and Terry Caldwell, when they argued about property lines, after Robinson built an access road.

That fall Izabela Lewicka literally disappeared off the face of the earth. It would be another year before her naked, decomposing body would be found stuffed in a fifty-five-gallon barrel on John Robinson's farm.

Over the next few months Izabela's parents in Indiana received letters signed by their daughter, enthusiastically describing her travels around the world. And if anyone happened to ask Robinson what had happened to his "niece" he would explain how she had been arrested for drugs and deported back to Poland.

In the spring of 1999, a couple of months before Izabela Lewicka disappeared, John Robinson invited his lifelong friend Mary White (not her real name)—whom he'd met as a teenager in Canada—to come and live with him in Kansas City. Seven years earlier, after hearing nothing from John Robinson for twenty years,

Mary's parents received a strange letter, purporting to come from Robinson's son. The letter—which was forwarded to Mary, now living in England with her third husband—explained that Robinson had never married and had adopted his brother's children after his brother had been killed in a car crash.

Since then Robinson and White had regularly talked on the phone, exchanged e-mails and become close. He told her that he held an important job with the CIA and was often on top-secret undercover assignments. Mary was impressed and now, as her third marriage had just ended, she agreed to his proposition, thinking that perhaps they might find true love together after so many years.

In June, Mary flew across the Atlantic to Kansas City and Robinson temporarily put her up in a suite at an extended-stay hotel in Lenexa. A month later, after the death of Izabela Lewicka, he moved Mary into the same furnished apartment in Overland Park where Izabela had lived. Throughout this time White considered Robinson the perfect gentleman, although he never discussed marriage or even stayed the night, saying that his work for the CIA was "demanding."

"I wanted him to be there more than he was," she would later admit.

In July, the two moved into an unfurnished duplex in Overland Park, as Robinson explained that he had recently downsized his house and had a lot of furniture in storage. A few days later Robinson arrived with hundreds of books on witchcraft and the supernatural, many of which had come from Izabela Lewicka's collection.

Over the next nine months Robinson rarely visited the duplex more than twice a week, never once staying the night. They only ever went out on two occasions: once to have breakfast and another time to buy a stun gun in her name across the Missouri border, which he said he was buying for a colleague.

Mary had no idea she was being used as a pawn in his dangerous game. If things ever got too hot and he had to go on the run, she would be his means of escape.

CHAPTER 16

SUZETTE TROUTEN

By February 2000, John Robinson was engaged in so many relationships over the Internet, that he was having problems keeping pace. As security, he apparently deleted all his e-mail every few days, and was constantly having to ask his slaves to re-send telephone numbers, frequently forgetting their personal details. To save time he often sent the same e-mails to all his slaves simultaneously, changing only the names.

As "James Turner" was consoling Lauralei over her brother's death, Robinson had also allegedly become Master to at least three other women: a psychologist from Dallas, Texas, a businesswoman from the Midwest and a home health care worker named Suzette Marie Trouten, from Detroit.

A small-town girl who had grown up in Monroe, Michigan, Suzette was the youngest of five children and the baby of the family. Born on April 13, 1972, she was fearless from the very beginning. At the age of two she first got on a horse to learn to ride and developed a life-long love of animals.

When she was eleven years old, her parents, Harry and Carolyn Trouten, divorced, and Suzette and her brother Michael stayed with their mother, as their other siblings had already left home.

Her parents' divorce left a lasting scar on Suzette. She developed a fierce, independent streak, which soon landed her in trouble with her teachers at Airport Grade School, as she always wanted her own way.

"She was quite a problem," said her mother. "She

thought she should be able to do everything the older ones did and didn't understand why she shouldn't."

In the mid-1980s Suzette, who had grown into a thin, attractive brunette, attended Jefferson High School, a few miles north of Newport, where she excelled in art. But the troubled girl had been deeply hurt by her parents' divorce. Later she would tell friends that as a child she had been sexually abused by an adult.

"[She] had some emotional problems," said her eighth grade English teacher, Sandy Yorker. "I thought she was a nice kid."

In 1989, at the age of seventeen, Suzette left Jefferson High after her junior year, telling her teachers that she wanted to be a nurse. For the next two years she worked for local fast-food restaurants to support herself. She loved her new-found independence. For the first time in her life she had her own money, and bought a computer.

Then Suzette started dating a local boy and fell in love. But when the relationship broke up Suzette was devastated, and fell into a deep depression.

One day she was talking to her mother in the living room when she suddenly pulled out a gun that she had borrowed from a friend, and shot herself in the stomach. She was rushed to the hospital but luckily it was only a flesh wound and there was no permanent damage other than a large, unsightly scar. Later she would tell friends that it was from a cancer operation.

"I don't think she tried to kill herself," said her sister Kim, who is fifteen years older than Suzette. "She was just being dramatic."

In August 1971, Suzette found a job as a nurse's aid at LaPrad Homecare in Monroe, where Kim also worked. It was a demanding job, caring for terminally ill patients at their homes but Suzette's compassionate nature made her excel. Her boss, Sharon LaPrad, said

she assigned Suzette the most difficult cases as she was
so good with the patients.

"She gave so much," said LaPrad. "She could handle
it mentally and physically."

Suzette found that she had a gift for nursing and decided to make it her career, studying nights to prepare
her for the exams needed to become a registered nurse.
She also took a second job for some extra money, working the evening shift at Bob's Big Boy restaurant, where
her mother did the day shift.

At the age of twenty-one, Suzette moved out of her
mother's house and found herself an apartment nearby.
Initially she lived by herself but later took a roommate,
named John Stapleton.

Now away from home, she remained close to her
mother. They talked every couple of days and she went
home for dinner at least once a week. But working two
jobs and studying at the same time proved highly stress-
ful. At night Suzette often had trouble winding down
and falling asleep. So she started going on the Internet
in the early morning hours and became fascinated by the
world of bondage and domination, which she had never
dreamed existed.

She began to experiment sexually with local men and
women whom she had met over the Internet. She found
herself a Master named Bill Regan (not his real name),
who lived near her. Regan, a police officer instructed her
in the bondage lifestyle, and they would often go out
with like-minded couples they met in BDSM chat rooms.

Suzette was soon drawn to Gorean-style BDSM,
which involved fantasy role play in chat rooms. Inspired
by a series of twenty-five science fiction novels set on
the planet Gor, written by a philosophy professor named
John Norman, Gorean has no rules. It requires a deeper

form of submission and does not have the safe, sane and consensual guidelines of regular BDSM.

Since the Gor books were first published in the 1960s, they have achieved a dedicated cult following and, although they are now out of print, are much sought after by collectors. On Gor—known as Counter-Earth for its orbit opposite Earth's—all women are slaves who must obey men and fulfill their every sexual desire. Gor has an enormous presence on the Internet and Suzette became a regular visitor to the Silk & Steel Website, where she played in a channel called Port Kar.

In summer 1996, Suzette met a Canadian woman named Crystal Ferguson (not her real name) online, who shared her devotion to Gorean bondage and agreed to teach her how to better please her Master.

Crystal, who lived in Halifax, Nova Scotia, played the part of "Seka," who was the first among slaves, responsible for training Port Kar slaves.

"Both of us enjoyed Gorean," explained Crystal, who was four years older than Suzette and married with two young children. "We were both sex slaves and served Masters together. I thought of her as my sister of the collar."

The two women soon bonded online, chatting for hours each day on ICQ, an Internet site that allows messages to be exchanged in real time. And within a few weeks the two women decided they were soulmates, giving each other pet nicknames, "Brat-Bitch" for Suzette and "Musky" for Crystal. They declared themselves sisters and began playing in various BDSM chat rooms together as a team.

Over the next few months, Suzette began to move away from the Internet, preferring the added excitement of real-life sexual encounters. Crystal began to worry about the risks her friend often ran, meeting strangers from the Internet for S&M play sessions.

"There were at least three men who lived in her area," said Crystal. "It was like [she] would go out on a date, but her dates didn't end with dinner. She entered into it knowing that he was not going to take her to a movie and then home, give a kiss on the cheek and leave. It was not that kind of relationship and she was an adult and knew it."

Whereas Crystal wouldn't tolerate a bondage partner physically hurting her, and would end the relationship, the more adventurous Suzette had no such qualms.

"She would go back over and over," said Crystal. "It's almost like she was seeking something that she couldn't find. She would go all the way."

Suzette's behavior was becoming increasingly extreme. She had her nipples, clitoris and labia pierced at the same time and then boasted of doing her bellybutton herself at home with a needle.

"It was stupid and I just couldn't comprehend what she was doing to herself," said Crystal. "When she had her labia done she actually hemorrhaged for thirty minutes."

In August 1998, Crystal made the first of two trips to Detroit, staying at Suzette's apartment. They became lovers, even taking part in BDSM sessions together with some of Suzette's local bondage friends. While she was in Michigan, Crystal met Suzette's mother and sister, and the two women's relationship deepened.

Crystal sensed Suzette was lonely and troubled and looking for love in all the wrong places. Sometimes she would become so depressed that she'd cry on the computer to Crystal, sobbing about her four miscarriages and how her life was "hell."

She often said her only consolation were her two pet

Pekinese dogs, whom she loved more than anything else in the world. She called the female Peta, her queen, and the male Hari, her king, and always carried them in a large shoulder bag, where they would peek out the top.

"Suz was really lonely and just looking for the ideal person," said Crystal. "I know she went through men like licorice but she was always looking for something she couldn't find in that person. There was always a flaw. She just wanted someone to be there for her."

In the spring of 1999, Suzette, now twenty-eight, first met "JR" online in a Silk & Steel Gorean chat room and was immediately charmed by him. JR told her about the new Website he was developing for The International Council of Masters and she offered to help him build it.

She became fascinated by the underground secret society that had been operating since the 1920s, and began trying to produce a Web page to do it justice. As an experiment she first set up an Internet site called "Gorean Slavegirl," with naked pictures of herself as an explicit photo-guide to the Gorean lifestyle.

Suzette had always been attracted to older men and thought JR's masculine grandfather look was very sexy. Over the next few months she told him about her troubled life and her frustrations at work. Once again JR portrayed himself as a wealthy Kansas City businessman and farm owner. He said he had recently taken over several companies from his elderly father, who had retired because of ill health.

Then he mentioned that he needed a nurse to take care of his diabetic father, during the round-the-world sailing trip they would soon be leaving on. He told Suzette she would be perfect for the nursing job, which paid $65,000 a year and came with an apartment and car.

Suzette was flattered and couldn't believe her luck.

She often struggled to survive on the $20,000 she earned in her two jobs. This would solve all her problems and be an all-expenses-paid trip around the world, and she would be able to save.

But she was street-wise and told JR that although she was interested, she needed to come to Kansas to meet him and his father and see what the job entailed. JR agreed this was sensible and invited her to fly out for a job interview, offering to send her return air tickets to Kansas City and pay all expenses while there. He also said she could bring Peta and Hari with her, saying they would enjoy the trip.

Suzette told her mother and sister about the dream job, carefully omitting the fact that she had met her prospective employer in an S&M chat room.

"It seemed too good to be true," said her sister, Kim Padilla. "I thought she had got the job offer through LaPrad Homecare, where we both worked."

When Suzette excitedly told Sharon LaPrad that she was interested in the new job, and what it paid, LaPrad too was highly skeptical.

"I said, You must be kidding," said LaPrad. "Are you sure this is on the up and up? She told me that she had met [him] through a nurse-placing agency, run by the wife of a doctor friend of hers."

Suzette explained that she was taking the precaution of first going to Kansas to meet everyone involved and would get a contract. LaPrad then gave her blessing, even lending her $350 in case she ran into difficulties.

But Suzette knew that Crystal would never approve of her working for a Master, so she never even mentioned it to her. She covered her tracks by saying she was going to Kansas with her boyfriend, Bill Regan.

. "She knew I'd freak," said Crystal some months later. "She wasn't doing safe things and it was wrong."

In October 1999, Suzette spent five days in Kansas City with JR, and later told family and friends all about it. Amazingly, he had apparently stage-managed the whole thing, as an elaborate sting, recruiting various friends and contacts to impersonate members of his family to draw her deeper into his web of deceit.

He had a limousine waiting at Kansas City International Airport to collect her when she arrived. First he showed her the mansion he said he lived in. Over the next few days he introduced her to his elderly father (his real father had died ten years earlier), a woman he said was his wife and several young women, who claimed to have also worked for him as nurses, saying he was a wonderful boss. He also showed her a furnished apartment in Overland Park that she could live in while they were home from their travels.

While she was in Kansas, Suzette also became JR's sex slave, allowing him to photograph them both naked in various sexual positions. Later she would e-mail the pictures to friends, boasting how good he was as a Master and lover. But although Suzette enjoyed being his slave, it was the high-paying job she was most interested in.

A month later she returned to Kansas to sign the contracts for the job and to arrange for her rental car. JR—who again footed all the bills—was more charming than ever, as he told her the itinerary for their upcoming trip, which included Hawaii, the Far East and Europe.

Suzette arranged to move to Kansas permanently at the beginning of February and begin work.

CHAPTER 17

LIKE A LAMB TO THE SLAUGHTER

SUZETTE Trouten had never liked Christmas, as it always reminded her how alone she was in the world. She much preferred Halloween, which she felt far more attuned to. Over Christmas 1999, JR was especially sympathetic, telling her how special Christmas was to him and his annual present-giving visits to the homeless. Next year, he promised, they would celebrate together in far off lands.

Over the holidays Suzette kept busy, preparing to move to Kansas. There was so much to do and so many loose ends to tie up in the six weeks before she was due to leave. She moved out of her apartment and back into her mother's house, so they could spend time together, and shipped most of her stuff to Kansas. Her considerate new boss had even agreed to rent her a small truck that she could drive Hari and Peta there in, so they wouldn't have to fly.

Then she gave her notice to Sharon LaPrad, after repaying the $350 in cash she had earlier borrowed.

"[Suzette] was very excited," remembers LaPrad. "She said it was a gravy job and not to worry because it was not forever."

All her friends were concerned for her, saying it sounded too good to be true and there had to be a catch somewhere. But they had to admit that JR definitely seemed on the level, having already paid for her two trips to Kansas City and all her expenses.

Finally she told Crystal, who sensed something was wrong with the set-up and urged her not to go.

"I was suspicious from the beginning, but what do you do?" said Crystal Ferguson. "I thought, How are you going to contact me from a ship? You don't have a laptop, you have a computer which won't work on a boat. She kept saying everything would be fine."

For Suzette, one of the hardest things about going was leaving her long-time boyfriend and Master, Bill Regan, whom she was in love with. Eventually the pressures of her going for an indefinite period put too much strain on their relationship and she broke it off in January.

Every day JR either e-mailed or telephoned Suzette, dispensing advice and discussing his father's health and their upcoming trip. He told her that it was essential she have the International Council of Masters' Website up and running by the time she arrived.

Each day she would spend hours on ICQ, instant-messaging Crystal with a running commentary of her sad and lonely existence, writing of her hopes and fears of leaving Monroe for the first time in her life. As her departure date grew nearer, she became ever more concerned about leaving family and friends. She lost her appetite and hardly ate, spending much of the time distracting herself with sex and trading pornographic pictures with Crystal.

On Thursday, January 20, her computer started freezing up and she was traumatized. But the following day, after fixing it, she wrote Crystal of a new "awesome" electrical sexual device she had purchased off the Internet for $500.

"It's the coolest toy I ever had," she announced triumphantly. "No burning flesh, no pain. It controls muscles. I have never cum like that in my life."

Later that day she complained that JR hadn't telephoned her as arranged to tell her when to set off for Kansas.

"Yesterday his secretary called me and said he would call," she ICQed Crystal. "He better hurry up or I'm going to get cold feet."

When Suzette admitted having second thoughts about going, Crystal advised her to abandon the job.

"My days are numbered baby," she wrote. "I have to go . . . money as usual."

By the following day, JR had still not called Suzette and she was very depressed. Attempting to cheer her up, Crystal asked if she was excited about going to Kansas. Suzette replied she was "scared" because "it's a long way from home."

On Sunday, January 23, JR left a phone message at her old apartment for her to call. But by the time her ex-roommate John Stapleton gave her the news, JR had left his trailer and all she got was his voice mail.

She spent a sleepless night worrying about the trip, but early Monday morning JR called, telling her to leave for Kansas on February 11. He said her apartment was all ready and gave her an itinerary.

"I will be there for a month and then I'm off to Europe for a few weeks," she excitedly ICQed Crystal, adding that they would be visiting Switzerland and Holland. "Me and Mom get [the] next week and a half together and then I go."

Suzette then promised to use her first wage check to fly Crystal to Kansas to see her, saying that the $65,000 that JR would pay her would be more than enough to pay off the bills she owed and pay for a vacation.

She also reported making good progress on the International Council of Masters' Website, where she had now set up a members' bulletin board and chat room under JR's instructions. Signing herself as "Webslut" and "Suzz Slave," she posted this message to new members.

I would like to thank each member for joining the ICM message board and hope as the site grows there will be many topics up for discussion and many questions asked so that we can all learn from each other . . . kisses suz.

A few days later, Suzette posted her own personal feelings of ambivalence about BDSM, in response to a question about the problems of having two masters at the same time.

Hello A/all. I was asked a question the other day and have been pondering the answer. How do you reply to someone who asks about BDSM and they have never been a part of it in any form? How would you explain the lifestyle to someone who wants to understand but is not sure if they can? Even after 12 years, I am still not sure how to bring up the subject to someone who isn't in the lifestyle but asks questions of it. I have seen so many people react with—you've got to be joking! Or that's sick! I am hesitant to really say too much on it . . . Just wondering suzz.

Later that day Suzette ICQed an Australian friend of hers named Ahsa, saying that her new job would soon take her to Australia, as JR had business over there.

"I want a wallaby," she told Ahsa. "I think it will be fun."

By Monday, January 31, John Robinson was apparently also making his own preparations for Suzette's arrival. He gave her his post office box number—100066—at the Crossroads Shopping Center in Olathe to use as her Kansas address. But when she gave it to Crystal, who had a present she wanted to mail her, she was unsure how to spell JR's last name, saying it might be "Robi-son." Finally, she told her just to send it in care of "John R."

Suzette was careful not to tell her friends she had become JR's slave. But after telling Ahsa how the new job, and the extensive traveling involved, had split up her relationship with Bill Regan, she coyly hinted that she would have a new Master when she moved to Kan-sas, emphasizing that it wouldn't be her new employer.

"[I'm going] for the job," she wrote, "but I do have a Master sort of close to where I will be and we talk regularly . . . grins."

The following day Suzette went shopping at Penny Pinchers to purchase a new set of clothes for her travels. She bought a second-hand full-length leather jacket for six dollars, leather boots for three dollars, a bustier, and a pair of wide see-through harem pants.

"I wanted a cool outfit," she proudly told Crystal, adding that she had also ordered a surgical steel branding iron, so JR could burn a floral rose on her ass. When Crystal asked why she didn't just get a tattoo, Suzette explained: "I want the brand done and over in two sec-onds—damn [tattoo] takes hours." She also said she was planning to write a piece on the ICM Website on the "branding issue" as a "mark of ownership."

But Suzette's mood had changed drastically by Fri-day, only six days before she was due to leave for Kan-sas. She said she was on her period, feeling confused and moody.

"It finally sunk in," she told Crystal. "I did some cry-ing."

Crystal then asked her what JR was like as a person.

"He is a good man," Suzette replied. "Very caring and extremely nice . . . I like him a lot. It should be OK after I get used to being there."

During her final week in Michigan, Suzette embarked on a crash diet. She started a three-day fast, only drinking fruit juice, saying she wanted to lose fifty pounds as she now weighed 180.

Within a day she began getting stomach cramps and diarrhea, saying that she felt like a "balloon," but was pleased that JR had delayed her trip by three days, saying he had to go out of town on business.

That Saturday, one day before she was to pick up the truck JR had rented for her drive to Kansas, he told her to expect to be abroad for at least six months.

"It's going to kill me," she ICQed Crystal. "I will miss my mom and Bill badly."

When Crystal told her that she had a "bad feeling" about the job, Suzette reassured her, saying she had even had JR checked out by some friends of hers in law enforcement.

"Don't worry about the job," she wrote. "That is the least of my worries. I will get to see places I have never seen. Like New Zealand, Europe and Australia. Places I could never afford to go."

She had promised to send her mother a doll from each exotic place she visited and asked Crystal what she wanted, suggesting maybe slave collars.

"Baby if this job works out I will be set for a long time to come," she wrote. "I won't be working much at all. Hey, sometimes fairy tales do happen."

Then Suzette, who always checked her daily horoscope in the newspaper, sent her Aries prediction for the upcoming week, saying the omens were good.

"You may be pinching yourself to be sure you're not dreaming," it read. "New challenges are at your feet. All you have to do is pick up the cudgel and begin to battle your way to the top of the heap. If there are obstacles in the way of your goals, you're the very person to fight your way through. You should make tremendous headway toward powerful goals by next week."

On Sunday morning, a few hours before she set off with her dogs for the three-day drive to Kansas City, Suzette sent Crystal a final ICQ before she broke down her computer. The truck was packed with her clothes and she had stocked up on dog biscuits and a bag of bones for Peta and Hari.

"It's strange Sis, getting ready to go," she wrote. "I feel sorta [sic] lost. I am such a moma's girl."

CHAPTER 18

THE KILLING FIELDS OF KANSAS

SUZETTE Trouten arrived in Kansas City on the afternoon of St. Valentine's Day and JR was there to greet her with flowers. Unfortunately, he told her, the apartment was not quite ready, as he checked her into a suite at the Guesthouse Suites and Apartments, on the exit of I-95 and 95th Street, Overland Park, using his credit card. Then he had to leave but promised to return later.

The first thing Suzette did was set up her computer to tell everyone that she had arrived safely. She was very tired after her long drive and after feeding Hari and Peta she fell asleep on the queen-sized bed.

Over the next two weeks JR frequently visited Suzette in her room, where they renewed their S&M relationship. He took more photographs of them together in different sexual positions, some of which Suzette e-mailed to Crystal, providing explicit captions like "Sucking Master's Cock!"

At first Suzette hardly left her room, spending her time watching television or on the computer. Twice a day she would walk the dogs around the motel, but there were few shops or restaurants within walking distance, and she had no transport after returning the rented truck. She telephoned her mother once a day and sent regular ICQs to her sister, Kim, Crystal and other friends.

But before long Suzette started getting homesick and restless. Every time she asked JR when she would be starting her new job with his father he hedged, making various excuses. He said he was busy on a new business venture but told her not to worry as they would soon be leaving for Australia.

Three days after she arrived in Kansas, Suzette ICQed Crystal, complaining she felt like "a caged cat." Her only trip outside the Guesthouse had been to take Hari and Peta to a dog-grooming salon. Then she had dropped them off at a kennel JR had fixed up for them, as the motel did not allow pets in the rooms.

On Friday, February 18, Suzette was feeling lonely and displaced, wondering when her fabulous new life was going to start. She had virtually stopped eating and was now existing on carrots and fruit juice.

"I'm going stir-crazy walking on the ceiling," she wrote Crystal. "I'm not used to sitting and it's making me totally nuts and I have PMS to top it off."

Her friend advised her to go out and get drunk. Suzette replied she had already considered getting a taxi to a bar but did not want to pass out butt-naked on the bed to be found by JR in the morning. "It's not good to moon the boss," she joked.

By the next day Suzette's mood had sunk even lower. She told Crystal that she wanted to go back to Michigan and that she felt "so anxious" that her head was about to "explode." She had just finished a heavy two-week menstrual period, describing it as "my vampire weeks."

Then she had to go as she was expecting JR to arrive any minute, so they could discuss her duties when she officially started work the following week.

That night Suzette was jubilant. JR had just left her room and they'd spent the day playing in bed.

"Just so you know I have the hots for my boss," she ICQed Crystal, who now had all her worst fears realized. "He is a Dom [dominant master] too. Did you expect me to work for a normal person? This is me we're talking about."

Shocked by what she'd heard, Crystal warned Suzette to keep her relationship purely business, or she would never be paid. Suzette laughed, telling her friend that having a Master on the upcoming cruise could be fun. Anyway, she had a signed job contract.

One week after she had arrived JR told her to prepare for their first trip. He informed her they would be driving to California in his station wagon and then sailing to Hawaii and on to Australia on his luxury yacht. They would leave at the end of the week and be away two to six months.

It would be Suzette's first time overseas and she felt a mixture of apprehension and excitement. She was especially delighted about the prospect of eating her favorite Thai food in California, before they set sail on his yacht. She had already sampled the local Thai food in Overland Park, declaring, "It sucks."

That morning JR had taken Suzette to the kennels to visit Hari and Peta, who were being groomed and having their hair braided when they arrived. She was glad that her new boss loved pets, and he had assured her they could come on the cruise too. Although there wouldn't be room for her computer on board the yacht, he promised she would be able to keep in touch with her friends and family through e-mail.

By Wednesday, JR had told Suzette that the trip was postponed. They would now be driving to Los Angeles in five days' time. "[I'm] just making sure I have everything settled so when I go I don't have to worry about anything," she told Crystal, adding she had a developed a new system to pay off her outstanding bills in Michigan.

The next day Suzette ICQed Crystal while she was waiting for her laundry to dry in the motel's washroom.

"I am a bad girl (grins wickedly)," she wrote, denying Crystal's accusation that she had just made love to JR. "I don't have much of a sex drive right now but teasing is fun."

Later that night she sent Crystal a chillingly prophetic poem. It began:

> *Here tomorrow, where are you going?*
> *Do you have some room for me?*

The poem looks forward to "a new day," but only if tomorrow "will have me." It speaks of a girl who has "been wanted," and who has "over-tasted" what life has to offer. Abused "by those close to me," Suzette returns to the refrain:

> *The night is falling and the dawn is calling,*
> *I will have a new day if you will have me.*

In a rare moment of introspection, Suzette told Crystal she felt confused and lost. Then she cryptically wrote that there was far more to her coming to Kansas than she had told anyone. When she was ready she would reveal what it was.

"I'm half excited and half regretful," she wrote. "I'm so excited to be here and going on the trip but when I made this move I knew it would change my life back home. I guess I'm trying to hold onto the past and future at the same time."

Then she explained that when she had accepted JR's job offer, she had known she would never return to her old life of poverty in Michigan. She said working with the terminally ill had aged her ten years in the last seven months and now she wanted an easy life before it was too late.

"I sold myself to the highest bidder," she admitted. "Do you really think after being pampered like a princess I will ever go back to working so hard I almost kill myself?"

When Crystal accused her of selling herself out to a "sugar-daddy," Suzette denied it, saying she had only come for the job.

"I'm a paid companion plus I do side-work," she snapped, "and the side-work isn't sleeping with anyone. If I wanted a sugar-daddy I could have stayed at home because I already had one, but I didn't want him."

Although she had already alluded to the fact that she had become JR's slave, Suzette told Crystal she was now trying to distance herself from him sexually and put their relationship on a purely business footing. It was a 180-degree turn from everything she had said two days earlier.

"I like him, can't say I don't. But I also now know that if I do it will screw this job up royally because he will expect it from then on. I hope ya don't think bad of me baby but this time money is talking."

Asked what her new job actually entailed, Suzette was evasive, saying: "I go places with John" and act as his personal assistant.

She claimed her other tasks included keeping track of his father's blood pressure and vital signs and looking into the logistics of setting up a home care company for JR.

"I do some computer work for him also," she wrote. "I'll more or less be keeping him company over the next year and go from there. It can be a pain in the ass at times."

By the following day, a Saturday, Suzette's attitude to JR had changed once again. After taking a long walk with him she now felt more optimistic, telling her Aus-

tralian friend Ahsa that they may even go on to New
Zealand, if there was good sailing weather.

"It should be real fun . . . grins expectantly . . . especially as I'm sailing with a Dom. I'm happy [that] I made
my move to Kansas City."

When Ahsa told her to have a wonderful time and be
careful not to fall overboard, Suzette joked, "With my
luck a shark will bite my butt off."

That night Suzette told Crystal of her concerns for the
health of her new boss. She was worried he was working
too hard and not getting enough sleep, as he was in the
midst of "a major business deal" to sell his company
before they left.

On Wednesday, the day before they were to leave,
Crystal begged Suzette to tell her the truth about what
she was doing in Kansas.

"You don't tell me about John or your job or day to
day things like you used to . . . What's up?"

Once again Suzette became evasive, writing that JR
lived in his own house and she was just doing his paperwork and shopping. She was also applying for a passport as well as sorting out her possessions, which would
either be put into storage or left at JR's house.

Astonished that she would be leaving stuff at her employer's house, Crystal challenged her, saying there was
something she was not telling her.

"There isn't honey," Suzette replied. "I promise baby
everything is ok. Actually things are going very good. I
am getting used to being away from home [and] not as
homesick as I was."

Crystal then mentioned that she planned to get her
nipples pierced and her Master had objected to her doing
so without his permission. Feeling mischievous, Suzette
then ICQed Crystal's master as a prank, telling him she
had already had the piercings done. To their delight, her

Master exploded, threatening to "flog" Crystal, who then told Suzette she was going to look for a new Master.

Late that night Suzette sent Crystal another cryptic ICQ after a visit from JR.

"God am I bad. Ya know I am going to do it. He is still bad ass, isn't he?"

At 10:30 a.m. on Wednesday, March 1, Suzette sent Ahsa one final ICQ before she broke down her computer, which would then be put into storage. JR had just called to say he was on his way to the Guesthouse to drive her to the kennels to collect Hari and Peta, as they were leaving first thing the following morning. But before they left he wanted to show her his farm in La Cygne so they would later drive there with the dogs.

Ahsa teased Suzette about seeing the world with her new Master, saying she would have a great time.

"It will be fun, baby," wrote Suzette. "We all finally find what we want and need and I found mine."

While she was still online with Ahsa, JR arrived at the door to collect her.

"Well sweets I have to run," she wrote. "I'm off to the farm this morning for a while . . . grins . . . love to you baby."

That was the last time anyone would ever hear from Suzette.

Later that day Olathe Animal Control Officer Rodney McClain received an anonymous call that two well-groomed Pekinese dogs were running loose at the Santa Barbara Estates. When McClain arrived he found the two dogs stretched out in a pet carrier outside Nancy Robinson's office.

"I found it kind of strange that those two real nice-looking dogs would be running loose over there," said

McClain, who was more used to dealing with stray cats or injured wildlife than immaculately groomed and well-fed pedigree Pekineses.

When he went into the office to investigate further, Nancy's assistant Alberta was "very sketchy" about where the dogs had come from. McClain then took the dogs back to his animal shelter behind Olathe Police Station and within days they were split up and given new homes by two local animal lovers.

CHAPTER 19

THE SLAVEMASTER

THE following morning, prosecutors would later claim, John Robinson took Suzette Trouten's computer to his trailer and spent the afternoon reading her e-mails, making careful notes of her passwords and address book, before erasing the hard drive. He then drove to Raymore, Montana, and put the computer in his storage unit, along with her clothes and other personal effects.

At 9:00 a.m. the following morning, Crystal Ferguson received an e-mail from *suzettetrouten@hotmail.com*.

> By the time you get this I [sic] off. My computer crashed yesterday and it took hours to get it working, you would laugh, station wagon full, the dogs in the back and off we go on the adventure of a lifetime . . . sees ya, Suz.

Believing it had come from her friend, Crystal replied that she had told her Master "to take a fucking leap" over him telling her when her nipples would be pierced. Now she was seeking a new Master. Within the hour she received a second e-mail from "Suzette."

> Caught your message just before I unplugged . . . If your [sic] interested in a MASTER who is really great, write him. He is a great MASTER. His email addy is *eruditemaster@email.com*. Wow, what news . . . I'm off, love you too, don't forget to write him!!!, hugs suz.

The next morning Crystal sent an e-mail to *erudite-master@email.com* and introduced herself, saying they had a mutual friend who thought they might get along. A few minutes later, an e-mail arrived from "JT," the initials of John Robinson's alias, James Turner.

> Crystal I understand you are a slave . . . I am a MAS-TER with 20 years experience. I am seeking a slave who is trainable. I understand that you just ended a relationship with your ex-MASTER.

JT then asked Crystal to describe herself, her "experience in the lifestyle," what she would be looking for in a Master. He concluded:

> When you reply, send me a picture of yourself along with your message . . . I await all the possibilities in front of us . . .

As a precaution, she then e-mailed "Suzette," asking what she knew about JT, adding that her old Master was furious she had "dumped" him.

The following Monday morning, Crystal received an e-mail from JT, offering to become her new Master and suggesting they meet if everything worked out.

"Slave: I understand the situation, Suz explained it to me before she made the suggestion. I told her to go ahead and drop you a note if she felt you were a good candidate. I am not sure how the travel will work, but I would like to explore it a bit more."

JT then warned Crystal that he would be a selective and demanding Master: "If I accept you, you will be my slave and you will understand your place is at my feet on your knees. There is no quarter given. I am firm but fair, I am stern yet caring. I am a MASTER who cherishes his slave!" JT concluded by insisting that Crystal e-mail him every morning before 9:00 A.M. Central Standard Time, and demanding an immediate rundown on her "bdsm experience."

Still not suspecting anything, Crystal e-mailed JT her picture, outlining her four years' experience in the BDSM lifestyle. She told him she had been "paddled, flogged, spanked and teased," but as yet she hadn't found the perfect Master "who makes my belly quiver."

JT immediately replied to Crystal, whom he now addressed as "slut." He told her he lived in the Kansas City area and complimented her on her extensive BDSM experience, promising to teach her "what a true MASTER" could do when they met in real life. Then he ordered her to send naked pictures and her phone number, so he could telephone her. "I take pics all the time so get used to it," he wrote.

That e-mail was soon followed by one from "Suzette," recommending JT as a highly experienced Master, who also happened to be a friend of JR. It said she had met JT in Kansas City, where they had all played together, before leaving for California. It described him as around fifty years old, 5'8" tall, weighing 185 pounds and "educated, very powerful and extremely dominant."

"I was introduced to him by my MASTER who by the way is the best fucking thing that ever happened to me in my whole life," read the e-mail, claiming to be from Suzette.

The MASTER you are writing to is a teaching MASTER who helps other MASTER's [sic] train their slaves properly. We are in Arizona now, moving toward California. Stopped at a café and they have this computer for rent. Having coffee and dropping you a note. Don't fuck this up, this guy will make your toes

curl and have you laying on your belly slithering to
him. Take care, I'll try to holler next time I see a
puter . . . Suz.

Still believing the e-mail to have come from her
friend, Crystal felt hurt and betrayed that she was now
referring to JR as her Master. She immediately replied,
accusing Suzette of lying and selling herself for money.
Within the hour an angry e-mail arrived from "Suzette," describing JR as her "knight in shining armor."

Figured you would fucking freak . . . I have found a
MASTER, and I have not been bought. Don't assume
things that are not correct . . . met this guy and he is
exceptional. Me and my dogs are ok with him, my
fat butt and all. He just recently finished selling off
his company and we are off to travel for awhile. I
have everything I need, so be happy for me damn it!
I love ya. When you meet him and we play, you'll
drool.

The e-mail went on to describe JT as a "real ethical"
mentor to his slaves, having put his last one through law
school, before releasing her to work for a large West
Coast law firm. It told her she should be honored that
JT would even consider becoming her Master, as he was
in such high demand.

On Tuesday morning, one week after Crystal began
receiving e-mails from JT, John Robinson apparently began getting confused by his own increasingly complex
scenario and started making mistakes. JT began answering questions Crystal had asked "Suzette," and vice-
versa.

On one occasion Crystal had e-mailed "Suzette" that
she was now contemplating having her nipples pierced

but then JT had answered, offering to do it himself, boasting that he had done hundreds of piercings. Another time she had mentioned to "Suzette" her intentions of finding other new Masters and unleashed a furious response from JT.

Crystal also noticed that "Suzette's" e-mails were all signed "Suz," something which she had never done before, preferring to use their pet names. And the word "Master" was also being spelled out in full capitals in both "Suzette" and JT's e-mails. Crystal checked Suzette's old ICQs and saw she had never used "MASTER" in any of them.

"I knew then something was wrong," said Crystal. "I'd send Suzette e-mails and he'd answer them—Hello, what's going on?"

At first she thought the mysterious JR might have sold Suzette into white slavery or prostitution. So she decided to play his bizarre e-mail game and try to draw him out, as he was her only remaining link to Suzette.

Over the next few days she exchanged sexually explicit e-mails with JT and "Suzette." With Crystal's wide knowledge of BDSM she was able to parry Robinson sexually, so he wouldn't suspect anything.

Then JT sent her the two pictures of a middle-aged, Stetson-wearing denim cowboy, relaxing on his Kansas farm. They were the same ones "James Turner" had sent Lauralei Meadows a few months earlier.

"Now you can see what I look like too!" he wrote. "Oh the third eye in the middle of my forehead has been covered with make-up, you know, my ogar eye ... chuckle."

Ordering her to put new batteries in her vibrator, he promised to take her to the "peace of the slave zone" and make her knees "buckle and turn to jelly," when they finally met.

On Wednesday, March 8, Crystal went on the offensive, e-mailing "Suzette" and asking what JR knew of her BDSM past.

"You've changed suz . . . you want me to fuck this up and tell this JT guy something by mistake?" she asked. "As for this JT . . . he won't answer any personal questions I ask him . . . NOTHING . . . He's already calling himself my Master and wants to pierce my nipples himself. I'm playing in total darkness here [and it] makes me very scared and nervous."

A few hours later JT wrote back, reassuring Crystal that Suzette was doing well and enjoying herself in California. He had also "dropped a note" to his friend JR, who had just updated him on their fabulous trip.

"Don't get so pissed at the girl," wrote JT. "She has found her MASTER and she is happy. From what I understand she didn't want anyone (her family) or the D/s community to know what she is doing. She had some bad, bad times in Michigan, now she is happy and on the adventure of a lifetime. So, be happy for her!"

Telling Crystal that he was "well versed in the Gorean lifestyle," he then outlined his future expectations for their master/slave relationship.

"As your MASTER, you will give me your body, mind and soul. I will own you and use you for my personal pleasure."

JT also asked for details of Suzette's sexual history and how many men she had been sleeping with before she had come to Kansas City. "I worry about the possibility of sexually transmitted diseases," he explained.

A few minutes later a new e-mail arrived from "Suzette," accusing Crystal of being "paranoid," asking whether she wanted a good MASTER who could improve her life or not.

"Now you bitch, open up to JT and tell him all. You will probably see the good side of him then, OK!"

After spending a sleepless night worrying about Suzette, Crystal decided to try to throw JT off-guard so he would make more mistakes. First she sent him complete details of Suzette's sexual history and lovers, including her policeman boyfriend and a Toronto judge. Then she contacted Trixie Gold (not her real name), a slave and mutual friend of theirs from Canada. She told Trixie of her fears for Suzette's safety and Trixie agreed to Crystal's new plan to give JT her e-mail address and see what happened.

Crystal e-mailed "Suzette," saying that Trixie would also like a new Master, asking if she knew one looking for a slave. A few hours later an angry e-mail arrived from "Suzette."

"Does [Trixie] think I am the clearing house for MASTERS," it said.

> Worried about me, ha! If you want to, you can give her JT's address, but I would tell him first what you are going to do. Or, a better way would be for you to give JT her address and tell him she is looking for a MASTER. He does know a lot of people in the lifestyle.

Later that day, after Crystal had sent JT her address, Trixie received an e-mail from "Tom," offering his services as a Master, using yet another e-mail address, *preipo@usa.net*. "Tom" described himself as a stockbroker, wanting full details about Trixie and what she wanted from a Master.

"I am a total MASTER," read the e-mail,

and what I require of my slave is "everything." I want
total obedience, total honesty and complete submission. I will use you. But I will also cherish you, care
for you and love you.

"So Trixie started helping me," said Crystal. "We
both knew something was wrong but how could we
prove it?"

Over the next week they continued to correspond with
JT and "Tom," who eventually gave Trixie three separate Kansas numbers where he could be reached by telephone, cell phone and pager. Then Crystal contacted
Suzette's old roommate John Stapleton to see if he had
her old telephone bills, so they could see if the numbers
matched. Stapleton said Suzette's mother had the bill
and refused to give out Carolyn Trouten's phone number, saying that Crystal was "overreacting" and it would
only upset Carolyn. Stapleton then mentioned that Suzette had told him that she was going to Kansas for cancer
treatment and had never spoken of a new job.

Frustrated by Stapleton's lack of cooperation, Crystal
then contacted Suzette's former boyfriend and Master,
Bill Regan, who was a police officer. A few days later
Regan checked out the numbers on the police computer.
Although the names were bogus, all the numbers led
back to John Robinson.

Every morning JT e-mailed Crystal a comprehensive list
of sexual assignments she was expected to perform that
day. Playing his game, she pretended to follow his instructions to the letter. He also started telephoning her
and would lash out in furious e-mails, if her husband
happened to answer the phone or if the line was busy.

At other times JT would display a kinder, gentler side,
telling her how much he loved her and that he wanted

them to be together soon. These calls made Crystal "shiver with absolute disgust," but she always remained cool, never revealing any distaste for him in her voice.

On March 15, JT e-mailed that he had just heard that Suzette and her Master were in California, making their final preparations before leaving for their two-year world cruise on his yacht. Suzette had sent word through her Master that she was having difficulty finding cyber-cafés, and would no longer be able to keep in touch on a daily basis.

"They have been out practicing sailing and Suz is taking sailing lessons, etc.," said the e-mail. "Don't worry, they haven't forgotten us!!!"

Minutes later an e-mail arrived from "Suzette" telling Crystal to stop "bitching."

> I have been on the move 24-hours-a-day, getting the boat ready for sailing, sailing every day, taking les-sons, learning . . . I will write more later.

Over the next few days JT started opening up to Crys-tal, mixing scraps of his personal life in with his increas-ingly hardcore sexual demands. He told her his real name was James R. Turner and he worked as the Vice President of Human Resources for a large corporation and was devoted to his children and grandchildren.

"I'm taking my daughter shopping today," he once wrote. "She needs a new attitude!! . . . and my slave needs a good whipping!"

On March 21, Suzette's family received an e-mail from her, saying she was about to embark on her great adventure.

"Well the wandering suz finally decided to drop everyone a note and say howdy," read the chain e-mail.

Sorry no e-mail up to now . . . no excuses just lazy. Peka, [sic] Hari and I are fine, they travel really well. I'm in California and getting rested up for sailing. Excited, what an opportunity. Promised mom I would send her a doll from every country we go.

I hope I didn't worry you at all, I really am having a great time, enjoying myself, I needed the change. Don't worry about me, I'm a big girl . . . bigger than I should be, Love to you all Suz.

Three days later, her aunt and uncle, Don and Marshella Chidester, received a further e-mail.

By the time you get this we will be off, I have written mom and dad each a letter so mom can quit worrying. Will not be on line for some time, but will keep all posted on the trip every chance I get. I'm excited, Peka and Harri [sic] have taken to boat life like they were born for it. At first I thought they would start their wandering and fall off, but no problems. Well aloha . . . I love you guys. Suz.

Carolyn Trouten knew immediately that the e-mail had not come from her daughter and something was "radically" wrong. It didn't sound anything like Suzette; the "phrasing" seemed all wrong and there were none of her usual spelling mistakes.

"Suz writes really fast and whatever she happens to get down is fine," said her mother. "Suz does not spell everything right and it wasn't phrased the way she phrases."

A couple of days later Carolyn received a telephone call from an anxious-sounding John Robinson. He told her that Suzette had suddenly quit her job to run away with a man she'd met in California. He then accused her daughter of using his bank card to steal money, telling her to ask Suzette to call him if she got in touch.

Carolyn was so traumatized by the bizarre telephone call that she told her daughter Dawn, who lives in Florida, to call the police. It would take Dawn almost a day to finally reach the Overland Police Department, where she spoke to a detective, who told her they were already investigating John Robinson in another matter.

Soon afterwards Carolyn received a call from a detective from the Lenexa Police Task Force, recently set up to investigate Robinson. He said he would be coming to see her within the next few days and asked her to collect all the e-mails received by friends and family since Suzette had left Michigan, as they could provide vital evidence.

When Suzette's sister Kim asked Crystal for all her e-mails, and the photographs of Suzette and JR together, she said she would do anything to help but was wary of exposing her "kinky secrets."

"If it helps finding her, it's worth it," replied Kim. "[Besides] it is really no secret, you know. She has told me everything. More than I want to know."

At the beginning of April, John Robinson asked one of his wife's Santa Barbara Estates maintenance workers, Carlos Ibarra, if he could get him four large oil barrels. Ibarra, who had helped Robinson transport a mobile home and a wooden deck to his Linn County farm a year earlier, asked what he wanted the barrels for. Robinson replied that he needed them for a fishing dock he wanted to build.

CHAPTER 20

STAKEOUT

WHILE JT and "Tom" were toying with Crystal and Trixie, John Robinson, police say, was also finalizing arrangements to bring other women to Kansas. In early March he reserved room 120 at the Guesthouse's sister hotel, Extended Stay America at the Quivera Road exit on the junction of I-435 and I-35, for the first of three stays.

On each visit he allegedly followed the same procedure. He always checked into the same room on the first or third floor for one week to ten days, using his credit card. Then a few hours later a woman would arrive with an overnight case to join him. She would then disappear into his room, where she would remain until they checked out.

Before long the motel management became suspicious of what was going behind the closed doors of his motel room. "One morning one of his women came down to my front desk person and asked him to make copies of something," said assistant general manager Brad Singer (not his real name). "One of the copies didn't go through the machine so he threw it into the trash can."

After he finished making the copies he gave them back to the woman, who took them back to the room. Curious, the desk clerk pulled the bad copy out of the trash and was shocked when he read it.

"It was a copy of a contract stating [that he] had full power over her mind and body and that he could do anything he wanted to her."

Kansas state law requires long-stay hotels to provide the police with a weekly list of the guests. So when a detective arrived for his routine check a few days later, he was given the signed slave contract. The detective seemed very interested, telling the manager to be sure to call immediately if Robinson made another reservation.

That spring Robinson's life was a hive of activity. When he wasn't on his computer, allegedly luring new slaves to Kansas, he was working on his latest business venture to put his modular homes magazine online with a sophisticated Website. In early March, he hired local web designer Steve Gwartney, meeting with him several times to discuss his ambitious new Internet project.

"He seemed fairly friendly and an outgoing type," said Gwartney, who agreed to design the site for $1,000. "He seemed very professional but didn't seem to know much about computers, but that was probably all a ruse."

Over the next few weeks Robinson wrote fifteen stories and editorials on the mobile home industry for the site, which was due to open in May. Designed to Robinson's precise specifications, Gwartney spent many hours constructing elaborate hyperlinks to trade associations and retailers all over America. But during telephone discussions, Gwartney often had to walk him through the basics of even locating his site on the Internet, as he claimed to be intimidated by computers.

Robinson was most proud of a link called "J. R.'s comments," where his own personal greeting message would appear with a logo of him grinning.

"He had a number of potential clients that were in the site but I don't know if they had ever agreed to terms," said Gwartney.

But when the site—*www.mmhl.com*—was finally finished, Robinson refused to pay the designer for his work and Gwartney took it offline after only a few days.

As the Lenexa Police Department placed him under close surveillance in late March, John Robinson was blithely unaware that he was even under suspicion. He now spent most of his time on the computer, scheming to bring more and more women to Kansas. And he was apparently becoming more and more confused by all the complicated scenarios he was constructing, explaining his mistakes by saying his computer had crashed and he'd lost phone numbers and other information.

During the last week in March "JT" and "Tom" told Crystal and Trixie to prepare to visit Kansas, suggesting that they might meet halfway in Chicago.

"I am trying to get a grip on how we handle this," wrote JT to Crystal. "You realize that you are going to fall in love with me completely don't you? Hugs, Kisses and Lashes, MASTER."

On March 29, Crystal received an e-mail from a detective at the Lenexa Police Department named Jack Boyer, urgently asking her to call him. He explained he was one of the lead investigators on a small task force trying to locate Suzette and needed her help.

"We are taking this very seriously," he wrote. "I have read your e-mails in regard to Suzette and think you can be very helpful in this case."

That afternoon Detective Boyer had a long telephone conversation with Crystal, who fully briefed him on the strange events since Suzette's departure for Kansas. The detective then asked Crystal to go undercover for the task force, saying she should maintain daily contact with Robinson and act as if nothing was wrong. He also wanted to see all Robinson's e-mails as she and Trixie received them, promising to guide her every step of the way.

Crystal was only too willing to cooperate. Although she had never liked the police, she was willing to make an exception if it would help find Suzette. So the next morning she e-mailed JT, saying she was ready and willing to come to Kansas as soon as possible.

"My kids would be home with hubby and I could devote some time to my Master," she wrote. "I know you'd enjoy it as I would . . . grins . . . licking her lips and thinking of a male g-spot."

An hour later JT replied, agreeing that she needed to spend some time in Kansas soon. He also mentioned that his friend Tom had not heard from Trixie in a long time.

"Hey, I'm just in a jolly mood," he wrote. "Tell me when you want to come to Kansas . . ."

Crystal sent the e-mails directly to Detective Boyer at Lenexa Police Department, asking if he wanted her to go to Kansas to entrap Robinson. Boyer replied that he was glad Robinson was still in contact, and obviously had no idea he was under surveillance. But he asked Crystal to continue playing him along and wait for further instructions before finalizing the Kansas trip.

The police now knew all about the FBI's abortive mid-1980s investigation into Robinson and how he'd been linked to the disappearances of Paula Godfrey and the Stasis. And they were treating it as a possible serial homicide investigation, under the watchful eye of Johnson County District Attorney Paul Morrison. But this time there would be no mistakes. Morrison wanted an iron-clad case against John Robinson so he wouldn't slip through the net of justice again.

It was a long, terrible April for Crystal Ferguson and Trixie, who continued their daily correspondence with JT and "Tom," pretending to be his willing slaves, always fearing for Suzette's life. There were days when no e-mails came, and they worried that Robinson had found them out. But the increasingly pornographic e-mails would always reappear, as JT explained that he was away on one of his frequent business trips or taking care of family matters.

"I'm here, I'm here," he e-mailed Crystal, after a three-day absence in early April. "Told you yesterday I was going to be out of town . . . grin . . . what's the matter, horny???"

At one point Detective Boyer sent Crystal a caller ID-Box for her phone to try to trace where Robinson was calling from. But his number was blocked. Most days the experienced detective, who was working around the clock with the task force, kept Crystal apprised of the investigation and even sought out her expertise on the BDSM scene.

On April 5, Detective Boyer reported that they had some "good leads" on Robinson, following the police visit to Extended Stay America and the discovery of his slave contract. But when Crystal asked his "candid" opinion of whether Suzette was still alive, the detective sympathized with her fears, refusing to elaborate on his own personal theories.

"I know you guys would like my opinion," he wrote, "but I've learned to be very careful and reserved when it comes to a case like this. I don't want to give up hope of finding out she is alive and well."

Three days later, after Crystal told JT she felt his feelings toward her had cooled, he replied it was "just the opposite.

"I have been trying to figure out when I can get you here . . . grin . . . I've been busy as hell with all kinds of shit happening and then a bit of laziness too . . ." he wrote, adding that today's tasks were "nipple training, tonight ice."

On Thursday, April 13, Boyer's partner, Detective Dave Brown, flew to Monroe, Michigan, and spent two days interviewing Suzette's family and friends. Admitting that things did not look good, he told them the daunting news that they had now located Hari and Peta.

"Then we knew for sure something had happened to Suzette," said Carolyn Trouten. "Suzie wouldn't walk five steps without her dogs. It was awful."

The next day JT told Crystal to start checking airline schedules from Nova Scotia to Kansas City and tell him what flights were available.

"Soon, my slut, soon, you will begin your training and be completely obedient to your MASTER . . . Just know I am thinking about you."

An hour later Crystal received news of a dramatic breakthrough on the case from Detective Boyer, who revealed that they now had hard evidence that Robinson was "definitely involved" in Suzette's disappearance, "one way or the other."

"This guy is an absolute con man," wrote Detective Boyer in his e-mail to Crystal, "and he probably conned Suzette to coming to Kansas on false pretenses[sic]"

Saying they still didn't know if Suzette was "just missing or worse," Boyer said the case was now being investigated as a homicide, as there had been no sightings or communications from her since March 1.

"That does not necessarily mean she is dead, but if we treat the investigation as though she was, we can get more cooperation from people, i.e. prosecutors, judges and possible witnesses. I appreciate you being candid with me and it does help me understand and will be beneficial down the road in a possible trial of this creep."

On April 19, Robinson apparently telephoned Crystal

in the afternoon and found that her line was busy. JT immediately fired off a ferocious e-mail, ordering her "to get off the damn phone so I can call you," telling her he had plans to soon "train that nice virgin ass."

On Good Friday, Detective Boyer returned to Kansas from a trip out of town and briefed Crystal on the latest developments in the investigation. That morning the police had asked Carolyn Trouten to page Robinson, so they could record the call and obtain a search warrant. Robinson called back, saying he had just received a postcard from Suzette and the man she had run away with, and was sure they were all right. But D.A. Paul Morrison still demanded more evidence before a warrant to search Robinson's trailer, farm and storage units could be granted.

Police forensic scientists had also been busy. They had found traces of blood in the Guesthouse Motel room, where Suzette had stayed with Robinson in February. Motel maids had reported blood on the sheets and towels on the three occasions they had cleaned the room during her stay. Although it was being tested, Boyer thought it was probably menstrual blood, from the heavy period she had complained to Crystal about.

"We don't have any of her blood to compare it with but they took some swabs and will hold it for DNA," he wrote.

The detective also told her of Robinson's "long past criminal record" and how he had served time in prison for financial crimes. But he refused to say whether Robinson had ever been accused of violence or abuse, adding that although he did not appear to work, he banked a lot of money twice a month.

"We know he has had contact with several different women in the past," he wrote. "Some of the contacts have been through e-mails and some through phone calls and/or personal contacts. We also know he has had girl-friends in the past."

Boyer said that he felt there was a "50/50" chance Suzette was still alive, believing that she was either dead or had been "sold off" to one of Robinson's contacts in the International Council of Masters.

Boyer rationalized that it defied logic for Robinson to spend thousands of dollars just to get her to Kansas for his sexual purposes. But he also felt certain that if she had been sold, Suzette was resourceful enough to have found a way to phone home or have someone do it for her.

"These things are what have us teetering," he told Crystal. "If you are hell bent on coming [to Kansas] let's work together and nail this guy."

About the same time Detective Boyer sent the e-mail, a nervous woman checked into room 120 at the Extended Stay America Motel and the police were waiting. They had had prior warning from the manager and had taken three rooms adjoining Robinson's, spending the previous day setting up cameras and surveillance equipment so they could monitor his every move.

The motel staff were told as little as possible and had no idea they were at ground zero of a suspected serial murder investigation.

Melissa Wright (not her real name) was a respected psychologist in her thirties from Dallas, Texas, and had just flown into Kansas City to spend a week with Robinson, whom she had met over the Internet a few months earlier. Recently laid off from her job in a nursing home, Robinson had promised to help her find a new position in Kansas City.

"They had been talking about playing with BDSM," said Marianne Castle of S&M safety organization Black Rose, who has a friend who knows Wright. "He had her pretty well."

Before departing, Wright had told their mutual friend about going to meet Robinson in an Overland Park motel room so they could play—and how she was bringing more than 700 dollars worth of torture toys with her for the rendezvous. Her friend told her she was crazy and it was far too dangerous to meet a total stranger in a motel room for sex. She finally persuaded the psychologist to set up a protective safety net, calling her every three hours while she was in Kansas City. If Wright missed a call the police would be summoned.

On Easter Sunday, April 23, John Robinson arrived at the Extended Stay America reception soon after Wright, and checked in to room 120. In place were members of the task force and the FBI, staking out the three adjoining rooms to gather evidence.

For the first couple of days Robinson played with his new slave, complimenting her on the array of exotic electric torture toys she had brought with her. She signed a slave contract and made her prearranged safety calls.

But on Thursday night, according to Wright's later testimony, Robinson brought out his camera and began photographing her tied up in various bondage positions. Wright ordered him to stop immediately and give her the film, as she did not wish to be photographed. She would also testify that Robinson then hit her hard in the face and continued taking pictures as she lay there helpless.

In desperation Wright told him that a friend knew exactly where she was and if she didn't make a prearranged call, the police would be summoned to the motel.

Robinson then ordered her to return to Dallas and start packing to move to Kansas City, where he promised to support her until she found work. He said he would arrange for a moving van to collect her belongings from her apartment the following weekend. Then Robinson left, saying he had to catch an 8:00 p.m. flight to Israel for a business meeting.

Wright then returned to Dallas and packed up her belongings but the movers never arrived. After telephoning Robinson several times in vain, she finally left an angry message on his answering machine, accusing him of using her, demanding that he return her sex toys.

According to Wright, Robinson then called her back in a fury and tried to blackmail her, threatening to send her slave contract and naked bondage photographs to the Texas licensing authorities and ruin her career as a psychologist.

"I got scared and that's when I called the police," Wright would later testify.

As soon as the Lenexa Task Force heard about Wright's complaint, two detectives caught the first plane to Dallas to interview her.

Late one night, about a month into the investigation, Jack Boyer was walking to his car in the Lenexa Police Department parking lot. It was a clear, late April night and he could see the stars shining brightly above Kansas City. Lately, he had found himself getting somewhat more emotionally involved in Suzette's disappearance than he usually did in a case.

Since speaking to the devastated members of her family and working with Crystal, he felt he had gotten to know the sad, troubled girl, who had believed John Robinson would make all her dreams come true.

By now he was certain she was dead and Robinson was responsible. And as he approached his car he looked up at the sky, pledging out loud: "We will get Robinson for you, Suzette."

CHAPTER 21

ENDGAME

WHEN the Lenexa Task Force heard of Melissa Wright's frightening Easter encounter with John Robinson, they called in the FBI. To their horror they now discovered that he had been suspected of being involved in prostitution and white slavery in the early 1980s. As the investigation moved into high gear, task force Detectives Boyer and Brown flew to Quantico, Virginia, to brief a team of FBI profilers on the John Robinson case. They had also asked a judge for permission to place a wiretap on all Robinson's telephone lines.

On April 27, John Robinson sent Crystal a bizarre new e-mail which blurred all boundaries between JT and himself, as if he no longer cared. It provided an elaborate new alibi to account for Suzette's disappearance, giving police their best evidence yet that he was responsible.

"Now, what I am about to ask you and tell you is to remain totally and completely confidential!!! You are to tell no-one is that clear," it began dramatically.

JT then claimed his accountant had recently discovered more than $10,000 of bogus charges on his credit cards, which were still in his possession. On investigation, he had discovered that someone had reported the cards missing and obtained new ones, using his Social Security number and other personal information.

"I believe it was Suzette who did it," wrote JT. "The companies are forwarding pictures from their cameras and bank ATM shots to my attorney."

JT claimed he had hired a private detective to investigate and now asked Crystal to supply him with all the information she had on Suzette's friends and contacts in Michigan. He was particularly interested in identifying the Toronto judge Suzette had once been involved in an orgy with.

Repeating that he did not want her to discuss this with anyone, he finished by saying he wished to finalize her travel arrangements to Kansas.

Crystal immediately sent the incriminating e-mail to Jack Boyer, who was most interested to read it. He immediately wrote back, calling it a significant breakthrough, as it confirmed that Robinson knew Suzette and still "hasn't the slightest idea" that he was under surveillance.

Boyer said the task force had two theories as to why Robinson was now accusing Suzette of fraudulently using his credit cards. Either he wanted to hide his money problems or was "trying to cover his tracks," by suggesting she had run off using his cards.

"Either way," wrote the detective, "we don't want you to provide him any information about her previous contacts. We think he will try to put this off on one of them if the heat hits him."

The detective added that they were considering having Crystal give him a "false name" to see if he would use it later, as they soon planned to approach him with "some general questions."

Suzette's aunt, Marshella Chidester, who was also in close contact with Boyer, was highly concerned that Crystal might be in great danger from Robinson if she went to Kansas City. She sent Crystal an e-mail warning her to be extremely careful.

"I talked to Jack [Boyer] and he's worried about you taking any chances on coming to Kansas," she wrote. "The same thing could happen to you."

Soon afterwards JT sent Crystal an e-mail telling her

he needed the information on Suzette's contacts immediately, as he was meeting his private detective tomorrow.

Just know that your MASTER thinks about you always and is getting to love his slave already . . . I
can't wait until you are kneeling in submission.

Crystal stalled and replied that she had the flu and
was too weak to research Suzette's contacts. He replied
that he knew she was "squeamish" but his PI definitely
needed the information by Monday. Then, ignoring
Boyer's instructions, she spent the next couple of days
compiling names of Suzette's BDSM contacts and sent
them to Robinson.

"I had to be honest," she would later explain. "Lies
only lead to trouble."

The last weekend in April, Robinson left Kansas City
for a family reunion to see his new granddaughter for
the first time. His sudden disappearance concerned the
task force, who were watching him around the clock.
They now felt he was "acting weird," speculating that
he may have turned the tables and have them under
counter-surveillance.

He returned on Tuesday, May 2, and sent Crystal an
e-mail picture of his new grandchild, thanking her for
the list of Suzette's BDSM contacts and cracking a rare
joke about his granddaughter's photograph.

Hi my beautiful slave . . . I just got back into town . . .
sent you an attachment. I've been with this girl you
see . . . Thought you should see her first hand so you
could really be jealous.

The following day Detective Boyer told Crystal he
was going to the library to research BDSM, asking what

books he should read. She wrote back, suggesting the *Sleeping Beauty Trilogy* by Anne Rice, which explicitly explores the life of a slave. But when Detective Boyer asked the librarian for Anne Rice books, he was told she had written seventy-two, and they knew nothing of the "Sleeping Beauty" series. These were in fact erotic early novels written under one of Rice's pseudonyms, A. N. Roquelaure.

Nevertheless, Boyer pressed ahead undaunted, purchasing a stack of books on sadomasochism and bondage, and began scouring them for clues to Robinson's deviant behavior.

Crystal also supplied the detective with her own guide to the Gorean lifestyle, even sending him some of her BDSM pictures, after getting a guarantee that she wouldn't be arrested.

"Bear in mind girl's like suz and me need this type of lifestyle same as you need water to live . . . it's a part of us," she explained to the slightly bewildered detective. "You are what we call vanilla . . . you do normal sex . . . missionary . . . we need dominance and pain . . . we need to submit to a Master . . . we crave it . . . apparently suz also craved a rich Master . . . she did not want to work . . . she got more than she bargained for Jack."

After seeing the bondage photographs, Detective Boyer admitted it was quite out of his scope of experience, adding that he had recently seen the Nicholas Cage movie *8MM*, and believed these things did happen.

"Yours is a very different lifestyle," he wrote, complimenting Crystal on her photographs. "But although it may be something I would not do, I try and keep an open mind."

A couple of days later, Crystal chided Boyer for getting his movies mixed up, explaining that *8MM* was about a snuff movie and had nothing to do with BDSM.

"Put me in my place . . . lol," answered Boyer, using the acronym for "laughed out loud." "Could have sworn I saw some sex in that film."

He then asked Crystal's permission to fly to Nova Scotia and interview her, so he could "learn much more about the lifestyle; more than what we can learn from books."

John Robinson was now e-mailing and telephoning Crystal daily, wanting her to come to Kansas as soon as possible. He told her he dreamed about "using" her and wanted her to "taste the flogger and feel the whip."

On March 7, Robinson had a family emergency. He told Crystal that his granddaughter was in intensive care for open-heart surgery, and he was looking after his other two grandchildren while their parents kept a hospital vigil. Crystal sent her condolences and prayers for the baby, saying his family was lucky to have him there to help.

"Wiggles my ass . . . horny as fuck for my sexy MASTER," she teased, "and knows it will be soon . . . smiles impishly."

Robinson replied with a pornographic bondage fantasy, involving tying her to a chair at a high-level business meeting and whipping her in front of his colleagues.

On May 9, the Lenexa Task Force formulated a plan to trap Robinson, utilizing Crystal's computer BDSM expertise. Detective Boyer asked if he and an FBI agent could come to her home and then have her go online, posing as another Master to meet Robinson in cyberspace and try to get him to incriminate himself. Crystal agreed to the plan and a trip to Nova Scotia was scheduled for the following week.

Two days later JT e-mailed her that his "grandbaby" was OK and was soon going home. He was also delighted to tell her that all the fraudulent charges had been removed from his account, as "the signatures were not even close." He informed her that he was now assisting the bank in a criminal investigation of Suzette.

Replying to the e-mail, Crystal said she was heartbroken that Suzette would do such a terrible thing. Then, in a highly risky play, she said she was certain Suzette hadn't the talent to forge his signature properly.

"I'm sure it's not like yours at all," she goaded. "She could barely spell . . . let alone forge and get away with it . . . stupid banks eh?"

Amazingly, Robinson never even spotted the bait. "It's a terrible thing . . . I really have heard nothing from her and don't expect to. As far as I'm concerned the chapter is closed."

Then he told Crystal not to fret. The only important thing was that he was "thinking" about her and "needing [her] in all ways."

There would be no further word from Robinson for the next five days.

By this time John Robinson knew he was under surveillance and had formulated a cunning escape hatch in case he had to go on the run. At his suggestion Mary White moved out of the Overland Park duplex in early May and back to Canada to care for her aging parents. Robinson had assured her that they could live a better life in Canada, where the US dollar went further.

"The plan was for me to join him at the end of June," she would later say.

But instead of his call, she would receive one from homicide detectives and learn the terrible truth.

On Monday, May 15, Detective Boyer told Crystal that the trip to Nova Scotia had been postponed. The task force had been tipped off that Robinson had another girl soon arriving in Kansas City and they were now on full alert.

"We are checking right now, as we speak," Detective Boyer wrote, "to see if she is perhaps, loading us a U-Haul truck. We will not let him take her anywhere."

The following morning a well-dressed lady arrived at Extended Stay America and checked into room 120, which had been reserved by John Robinson several days earlier. Virginia Dickson (not her real name) had been previously booked on Robinson's credit card. The well-dressed young accountant with dyed blonde hair had flown all the way from San Francisco to meet "The Slavemaster," whom she had been corresponding with for months in a BDSM chat room. She had willingly agreed to be his sex slave and would sign his contract, giving him ownership of her mind and body.

A couple of hours later, a casually dressed Robinson seemed in good humor as he signed in at the front desk and went to his room. The next morning, when Extended Stay America maintenance worker John Tinsley arrived at room 120 to fix the air conditioner, he found Robinson in bed with Dickson and her small dog. Robinson was furious at being disturbed and shouted at Tinsley, ordering him not to enter. He then demanded to talk to the manager.

"He seemed like a very disturbed person to me," said Tinsley. "He asked me why I had to come into his room, and I told him I had to fix the air conditioner and I pointed out that we didn't allow dogs."

After a heated argument with the motel manager, Robinson finally agreed to have his air conditioner repaired and to get rid of the dog.

For their week-long stay, Dickson would later testify, Robinson would arrive at the motel about ten o'clock at night and then leave again early the following morning.

Dickson would remain in the room the entire time she was there, except for leaving once to wash the laundry.

One morning, after Robinson had left, Brad Singer passed Dickson in the corridor and was curious.

"I said, 'Hi, how are you doing?' " remembers Singer, "and she kind of looked down at the floor and seemed distressed."

On Friday, May 19, according to court testimony, John Robinson went too far in a brutal BDSM session with Virginia Dickson. He overstepped the limits of safe, sane and consensual by photographing her against her will, bound and naked. When she objected, Robinson bristled with anger and ordered her to pack her bags and leave, abandoning her outside with no money for a taxi to the airport.

Hysterical and crying, Dickson then called the police to complain. She was placed in a safe house and then questioned for two-and-a-half days by the Lenexa Task Force before the FBI were called in to see her.

On Saturday, May 20, JT resumed his e-mails to Crystal, without any explanation for his absence.

> Hello my slut: Have you done your tit training today, clamped nipples and all? Tonight the ice training and, tonight I want you to insert the vibrator in my ass (do it slowly) then turn it on and complete the training, you will continue until you cum three times!
> I tried to call you yesterday, no answer . . . sob . . . beginning to think my slave is a mirage.

Two days later, Jack Boyer informed Crystal of recent developments in the case, saying he was leaving that afternoon for Texas to interview Virginia Dickson. He would then proceed to Arkansas to see another woman who had complained about Robinson.

"[We are] finally getting some breaks," he wrote. "We are hoping that the D.A.'s office is going to see this as a positive step in the right direction."

For the next week Crystal corresponded with Robinson every day, never letting on that there was anything amiss. They started finalizing her upcoming trip, but since his altercation with Virginia Dickson, he seemed to sense he was under some kind of surveillance.

He had recently installed several security cameras around his trailer home at the Santa Barbara Estates and put a new alarm on his truck, telling puzzled neighbors that there were prowlers around.

"It is a real busy time," he wrote Crystal on Wednesday morning. "[I] just have sooooooo much to accomplish and no time to do it. Need my slut with me."

On the Friday before Memorial Day, Robinson telephoned Crystal for phone sex, which she pretended to play along with. He told her he was making arrangements for her to come to Kansas within the next couple of weeks.

"I could talk to you for hours," e-mailed Crystal after putting the phone down. "I love your voice."

Over Memorial Day, Robinson organized Santa Barbara Estates' annual barbecue, as though he didn't have a care in the world. The task force had now grown to thirty officers and there was a small contingent hidden on the edge of the estate, watching his every move.

On Tuesday morning, Johnson County District Attorney Paul Morrison was fully briefed by the task force on the latest developments in the Robinson case. They were ready to pick up Robinson for questioning, as soon as Morrison gave them the go-ahead.

There was a feeling of frustration in the task force

that the methodical D.A. was not moving fast enough. But Morrison realized that this case could well set a legal precedent, involving a possible serial killer using the Internet as a weapon. He was prepared to be patient and wait to ensure there would be no mistakes when he finally made his move and arrested John Robinson.

On Thursday, June 1, Suzette Trouten's family all received computer-generated letters in the mail, bearing Mexican postmarks and Suzette's signature. Detectives would later discover that Robinson had given the letters to Santa Barbara Estates' maintenance man Carlos Ibarra's mother, who was visiting from Mexico, to mail on her return home.

The letters, in distinctive yellow-and-pink envelopes, said she and "Jim Turner" were having a wonderful time, sailing from port to port and how Peka [sic] and Hari happily stood on the bow of the yacht to bark at dolphins. She had even given up smoking, and life could not be more perfect.

The letter was immediately faxed to the task force and handed to D.A. Paul Morrison, together with a startling e-mail that Crystal had just received from JT.

ohhhhh, another glare!!! MASTER was busy as a skunk being chased by a pack of hounds, didn't even have time to stop and spray them with stink... grinnnn. Sorry, I was thinking about my slave very much... meetings, meetings, meetings.

Today my nipples need a bit of attention, see to it, also the balls in my pussy should ease the tension until you complete your ice training tonight... Love ya, Hugs, Kisses and Lashes, MASTER.

On reading the letter and e-mail, Morrison told the task force to move in and arrest Robinson.

* * *

That night, as Paul Morrison was rubberstamping his arrest warrant, John Robinson summoned Olathe police to report that he had been assaulted by a youth, after an argument over loud rap music. The police officers, who were unaware of the three-month task force investigation, took a sworn statement from Robinson. He told them that he had asked the seventeen-year-old boy and several others to turn down their boom box and they had begun threatening and shoving him.

The youth was then arrested for battery and taken to the Johnson County Juvenile Detention Center, as the poor victim commiserated with the officers about the falling standards of today's youth.

CHAPTER 22

CAUGHT

AT 10:15 a.m. on Friday, June 2, the task force finally moved in to arrest John Robinson in his trailer on the Santa Barbara Estates. Ten unmarked police cars surrounded 36 Monterrey Lane and two officers walked up to the front door and knocked. Robinson opened the door and was told he was under arrest.

He put up no resistance, remaining silent as he was handcuffed and read his Miranda rights. Then, staring straight ahead without a trace of emotion, he was led out across his immaculately manicured lawn to a waiting police car, to be driven to Johnson County Jail for processing.

Sara Khan was sitting in her front room at the time and only realized that her next-door neighbor had been arrested after her young son came in to tell her. She immediately walked across the estate to the manager's office, where Nancy Robinson, oblivious to what was happening, was still working at her desk.

"I asked Nancy if she was OK, as her husband had been arrested," said Khan. "She didn't know and seemed surprised. She told me she would check."

Within minutes scores of police and crime-scene experts converged on the Robinson trailer and began to take it apart, searching for evidence.

As curious residents watched the surreal spectacle going on at the manager's trailer, police photographers took pictures of it from every conceivable angle, and forensic experts dusted it down for fingerprints. Over the next six hours they brought out three desktop and two laptop computers, several fax machines and dozens of cardboard boxes, which were then taken away for analysis. Finally they towed away Robinson's pick-up truck.

Late that afternoon Lenexa detectives converged on Needmor Storage at 1702 North Kansas, where they had discovered that Robinson had rented out locker B-18 two years earlier. Inside the locker Lenexa Detectives Dawn Layman and Dan Owsley found a brown leather briefcase containing Suzette Trouten's Social Security card, birth certificate and passport application, as well as her signed two-page slave contract and a stun gun.

Lying next to the briefcase in a plastic box, detectives found Izabela Lewicka's college ID, Kansas driver's license and an unsigned six-page list of "basic slave rules." There was also a photograph of her lying naked on a bed with distinctive green diamond–patterned sheets.

Also in the locker were dozens of blank sheets of paper bearing the signatures of both Trouten and Lewicka, along with envelopes addressed to various members of their families.

A few hours later John Robinson was formally charged with the aggravated sexual battery of Melissa Wright and Virginia Dickson, and one count of felony theft of Wright's sex toys. Further charges were anticipated within days. John Robinson refused to say anything, exercising his right to see his lawyer. His bond was set at $250,000 and he was placed in solitary confinement at the Johnson County Adult Detention Center.

Nancy Robinson was also brought in for questioning, white-faced and stunned by the arrest of her husband. Later she was released after telling detectives she had merely suspected him of having an affair and nothing more. That night she went into hiding, never to return to the Santa Barbara Estates.

*   *   *

Early Saturday morning a team of detectives and forensic experts from the newly-named Missing Persons Joint Task Force, led by D.A. Paul Morrison, converged on John Robinson's sixteen-and-a-half-acre farm in La Cygne. They were in a somber mood as they began taping it off as a crime scene and setting up a crime lab.

On the south side of Robinson's land was an old trailer used for storage, with five enormous metal barrels standing upright outside it. The police cadaver dogs soon picked up a scent emanating from two of the sealed barrels and began barking excitedly.

There was tension in the humid morning air as everyone fell silent, focusing their attention on the barrels. Then the police forensic experts moved in, rolled out the first one, removed the seal and opened it. Inside was a naked and blindfolded decomposing female body, lying face-down in a fetal position.

The crime lab experts then opened the yellow eighty-five-gallon barrel next to it and found the remains of another naked woman, also wearing a blindfold of green diamond–patterned material. Detectives, who had been working the Robinson case for the last three months, immediately suspected one of the barrels held the body of Suzette Trouten.

A police photographer took scores of pictures of the remains and the forensic scientists began gathering evidence. The two bodies were then taken to the office of Linn County Medical Examiner Dr. Donald Pojman, in Topeka, for autopsy. Other evidence was taken to the Kansas City regional crime lab for forensic analysis.

The following day Morrison's office telephoned the District Attorney of Cass County, Missouri, Chris Koster, and asked him to prepare a search warrant for Robinson's two storage lockers in Raymore. That afternoon the warrants were signed by Missouri Circuit Court Judge William Collins, and plans were made to execute them.

On Monday morning D.A. Koster, Raymore Police Chief Kris Turnbow, and members of the task force team arrived at Stor-Mor For Less at 711 E. Missouri 58, to search Robinson's storage lockers. Koster watched as officers of the Kansas City Regional Crime Lab opened locker E2, at the far end of the third of four long rows of barracks-style lockers, surrounded by barbed wire.

On the front of his ten-by-fifteen-foot locker was a heavy padlock, bearing the initials "SM." Some wondered if it was an arrogant reference to Robinson's internet name, The Slavemaster.

"The minute I saw the three barrels I knew it was going to be a big case," said Koster, who had not had a homicide in his county for almost two years, the longest they had gone without one since the mid-1980s. Each metal barrel had been double-wrapped in heavy-duty plastic sheeting and there were open boxes of kitty litter nearby, which had failed to mask the foul odor emanating from the barrels.

The first of the three large black barrels, which bore the label "RENDERED PORK FAT," was carefully opened by Kevin Russell Winer, of the Kansas City Police Department Crime Lab.

"When I looked inside, there was a shoe, a light brown sheet, and a pair of glasses," said the criminologist. "I lifted up the shoe and apparently there was a leg attached to it."

The plastic-wrapped barrel was then resealed and loaded into a police van with the other two still-sealed ones, and driven to the office of Missouri Medical Examiner Dr. Thomas Young, in Jackson County.

"I kept telling the police that my Mr. Robinson and

their Mr. Robinson were two different people," said the Stor-Mor For Less manager, Delores Fields, who was closely questioned by detectives as the barrels were found, together with a computer, camping gear and household items. "I had thought he was a nice person."

The elderly manager, who is an avid true-crime buff, also provided a major lead for the task force. She told them how Robinson had spoke about storing furniture for his sister, Beverly, while she was in Australia. Before long they had made the connection between Robinson and former prison librarian Beverly Bonner, who had come to Kansas City to work for him six years earlier.

At the same time that the three new barrels arrived at Dr. Young's office, D.A. Paul Morrison held a press conference at Lenexa Police Headquarters. Flanked by Linn County Sheriff Marvin Stipes and Overland Park Police Captain Jeffrey Dysart, a stern-faced Morrison told several dozen print and television reporters about discovering the two bodies in barrels on the Robinson farm, saying that both women had been beaten to death with a blunt object.

"Mr. Robinson is a suspect in the deaths of the two women found in the barrels in Linn County," said the genteel, balding D.A. in his soft Midwestern accent. Although he did not name Suzette Trouten, he acknowledged that one of the bodies was believed to be an out-of-state woman missing since March 1. He refused to elaborate on the circumstances that had led to the women's deaths, adding that no one other than Robinson was expected to be charged in the case.

Sheriff Stipes then said police were still searching every inch of the farm and preparing to drain a pond on Robinson's land for more evidence.

Soon after the press conference, an impassive-looking

John Robinson was led into the Johnson County Courthouse, where his bond was raised to $5 million, the largest ever set in the county. Wearing a standard-issue orange prison suit, he tried to shield himself from a barrage of waiting photographers, holding a large manila envelope over his face.

That afternoon, as the press learned more about John Robinson's Internet persona, "The Slavemaster," there was a media frenzy. Scores of reporters converged on the Santa Barbara Estates and the farm, questioning anyone who had ever known the Robinsons.

At 5:30 p.m. that afternoon the three barrels found in his Raymore storage locker were opened by Dr. Young. Apart from the body discovered that morning, there were two more lying stuffed in the remaining barrels, in varying states of decomposition. As the autopsies began, D.A. Koster scheduled a press conference for the following afternoon.

On Tuesday morning, Kansas City awoke to the shocking news of one of the worst serial killings in state history. "Police Name Suspect in Deaths of Women," trumpeted *The Kansas City Star*, which would devote many front pages to the barrel murders in the weeks to come. *The Olathe Daily News* reported that Robinson, now being called "The Slavemaster" was believed to be involved in "sadomasochistic activity" over the Internet, and would soon be charged with the killings of at least two women found on his farm.

Kansas City's four main television stations all reported Robinson's long criminal record and how he had also been suspected in the disappearance of several women and a baby girl fifteen years earlier. It was the biggest story that had hit Kansas City in years and the media's interest was insatiable.

That afternoon, at a joint press conference with Morrison at the Cass County Courthouse in Harrisonville, Missouri, Chris Koster confirmed that the three barrels found in the Raymore storage locker each contained a female body. Koster speculated that the badly decomposed bodies could have been in the barrels for years.

"This started out as a missing person investigation," Morrison told the press, "but now this case has taken on a life of its own. In some cases we have names but no photographs, and in others we have photographs and no names."

Morrison then revealed that there could be as many as nine victims, admitting it was "impossible" to know where the case would end. Police were still at the Santa Barbara Estates, digging beneath the Robinson trailer, as well as at several other sites in the area, where the Robinsons had lived over the years. Florida police were also searching his property at Big Pine Key, which had been sold eighteen months earlier.

Late that afternoon public records relating to the 1980s investigation into Robinson were ordered sealed by the Kansas District Attorney's Office. These included reports by Missouri Probation Officer Steve Haymes, which would prove highly embarrassing to the FBI and the Overland Park Police Department. But a police clerk at Overland Park, who had not been told, handed them over anyway, to *The Kansas City Star* and several television stations.

On Wednesday morning the *Star* named one of the dead women found at the farm as Suzette Trouten, reporting her move to Kansas City for a new job with John Robinson. The story also went out on the national wires and made *The Washington Post* and *The New York Times*.

There was immense national and international interest

in the case, with its use of the Internet as a tool of serial murder. *USA Today* and the *New York Post* both agreed that if eventually found guilty, John Robinson would achieve the dubious distinction of being America's first cyber-sex serial killer.

That morning Paul Morrison's office issued a press release, under the auspices of the now-renamed "Robinson Homicides Task Force." It had swelled to more than thirty officers, including representatives of the Kansas Bureau of Investigation, the Lenexa Police Department, the Linn County Sheriff's Office and the Raymore Police Department.

"The investigation into this case continues at a rapid pace," began the release, which officially identified Suzette Trouten for the first time. It also linked Robinson to the 1980s disappearances of Paula Godfrey, Lisa and Tiffany Stasi and Catherine Clampitt. "Because of facts that cannot be discussed today, the cases were never successfully resolved. One thing, however, that is known, is that all three of these individuals had connections with John Edward Robinson, Sr."

It also asked for any information from the public about Izabela Lewicka, whose photograph accompanied ones of all the missing women.

On Thursday, June 8, John Robinson's court-appointed lawyer, Byron Cerillo, said that his client would be entering a not guilty plea to all charges. He told reporters that with all the publicity, Robinson would not be able to get a fair trial in the Kansas City area and that if Morrison had sufficient evidence, he would already have filed murder charges.

"They're saying he's a serial killer," said the public defender. "I resent [it]."

Still in hiding, Nancy Robinson and her four children issued a joint statement to the press, describing their situation as "surreal." The gossip on the Santa Barbara Estates' grapevine was that Nancy had finally washed her hands of her husband, and would not lift a finger to help him. Indeed, the tersely written family statement seemed ambiguous. On the one hand, John Robinson's family described him as "a loving and caring husband and father," but they also wanted to know the facts.

"We, as a family, have followed the events of the last week in horror and dismay along with each of you. As each day has passed, the surreal events have built into a narrative that is almost beyond comprehension. While we do not discount the information that has and continues to come to light, we do not know the person whom we have read and heard about on TV."

That night Kansas forensic investigators tested Robinson's Linn County farm for traces of blood and other evidence of bodily fluids with Luminol, a substance which illuminates the remains of bodily fluids in the dark. The tests proved positive and unspecified materials were taken to a Kansas City crime lab for further analysis.

Over the next week new revelations in the Robinson case broke daily in the Kansas City newspapers and television news. Teams of reporters fanned out all over America, searching for human interest stories on the increasing number of women now being linked to Robinson.

On Monday, June 12, Missouri D.A. Chris Koster officially identified the first of the three bodies found in the storage locker as Beverly Bonner. The body was in such bad condition that forensic scientists had to use dental records. The youthful D.A. said that he expected Missouri to charge Robinson soon.

The day before, *The Kansas City Star* had carried an in-depth three-page feature, with a headline asking:

"Who is John E. Robinson Sr.?—Eagle Scout. Businessman. 'Man of the Year.' Habitual Swindler. 'Slavemaster.' Serial Killer? The life of the man suspected in one of KC's most notorious murder cases has taken one extraordinary turn after another."

The feature chronicled John Robinson's astonishing life of crime and how Steve Haymes and the FBI had failed to end it fifteen years earlier. It was a damning indictment of Kansas City law enforcement in the 1980s, fully supporting the worst fears of the families of his early victims.

Bill Godfrey, whose daughter Paula was the first to go missing in 1984, says that at the time the police did little to find her.

"If I was to give my true feelings on the way the investigation was handled, my level of cooperation from the [present] police would be terrible," he said. "We did all we could at the time and there didn't seem to be many answers from the police."

CHAPTER 23

MEDIA FRENZY

ON Tuesday, June 13, John Robinson was charged with five counts of first-degree murder in Kansas and Missouri, with both states announcing their intention to ask for the death penalty. The Robinson Homicides Task Force also pledged to continue investigating the disappearances of Paula Godfrey, Catherine Clampitt and the Stasis.

That morning in Johnson County District Court, Robinson was formally charged with two counts of capital murder in the deaths of Suzette Trouten and Izabela Lewicka. He was also accused of a further count of the aggravated kidnapping of Suzette.

Later that day he was charged in Cass County Circuit Court with the murder of Beverly Bonner and two unidentified Jane Does. Earlier Koster had sent Robinson and his lawyer "death letters," a long-time Missouri legal custom for notification of the death penalty. The "death letters" stated that Robinson had committed multiple homicides "in a manner outrageously or wantonly vile, horrible or inhuman in that it involved torture or depravity of mind."

For both District Attorneys it was going to be an extremely high-profile murder case, ensuring national attention. And the stakes were high, as it was the sort of case that could make or break a prosecutor's career.

At a joint press conference that afternoon, Paul Morrison and Chris Koster stood side by side on a podium, fielding reporters' questions. With his chiseled features and bushy Civil War mustache, Morrison, who already had a number of celebrated murder cases under his belt, appeared the consummate professional, whereas Koster, just thirty-five, was comparatively inexperienced, having prosecuted few murder cases during his six-year tenure as D.A.

But the differences between them went even deeper, right back to the age-old rivalries between the two neighboring states. Now John Edward Robinson inextricably linked Kansas and Missouri together in serial murder, and each district attorney wanted to put him on trial first.

The son of a railroad man on the old Santa Fe Line, Paul Morrison had wanted to be a lawyer since he was a young boy. After becoming the first member of his family to go to college and graduate, he went to law school to fulfill his dream of becoming a prosecutor. During his three years at the Washburn Law School in Topeka, he interned for several rural Kansas prosecutors and by the time he graduated in 1980 he'd already worked on several hundred misdemeanor cases and actually prosecuted a few jury trials.

He was then hired by former Johnson County District Attorney Dennis Moore, as an assistant district attorney, and was elected D.A. in 1988, after Moore stepped down. During his twelve years on the job he had become one of America's most respected and successful prosecutors.

A year after becoming Johnson County D.A., Morrison prosecuted the landmark case of serial murderer Richard Grissom Jr., who murdered three young women during a two-week period. Although the bodies were never found, Morrison gained a solid conviction and made criminal history by getting a conviction in one of the first murder trials in America to use DNA as evidence.

Six years later he prosecuted the celebrated case of

tragic mother Dr. Debora Green, in which John Robinson's detective son-in-law, Kyle Shipps, had been involved. After Green confessed to setting her mansion
alight and killing two of her children, the case gained
international attention when best-selling crime author
Ann Rule wrote an excellent book about it, called *Bitter
Harvest*.

"Paul is very aggressive," said an experienced Kansas
attorney who has tried cases against him. "He's been a
prosecutor his whole professional life and I'm not saying
he would break the rules, but he will do what it takes to
win. He might even bend them just a little bit."

Ironically, Morrison's wife Joyce is a news director
at one of Kansas City's leading television stations. They
had agreed long ago never to discuss his cases, knowing
that it would be a recipe for disaster.

With almost unlimited resources at his disposal, Morrison works from a palatial office, occupying the whole
fifth floor at the Johnson County Courthouse in Olathe.
But things are very different for Chris Koster, who has
a tiny, cramped office in a small annex to Cass County
Court in Harrisonville, accommodating just two secre-
taries and his assistant.

Born in 1965 in St. Louis, Koster got an undergrad-
uate degree from the University of Missouri and then
went on to study law there in 1991. After graduating, he
spent three years working for the Missouri Attorney
General's Office and was then hired by a Kansas City
law firm.

In 1994 Koster was elected Cass County D.A. and
was reelected four years later. Deceptively laid-back and
gregarious, Koster's ambition soon won him a reputation
among local reporters as publicity-hungry. This would
prove a sore point during the crucial, early stages of the

Robinson case, as the two prosecutors worked together in an uneasy truce.

The general feeling among Johnson County law enforcement officers was that as the original murders had been committed in Kansas, and as they had found the bodies for Koster, it was their case. Without their three-month-long investigation Cass County wouldn't even have a case to try. Besides, Robinson was in custody in Kansas and there was no way they were going to hand him over to Missouri until they had finished with him, however long it might take.

The same day Robinson was charged with five counts of murder, Detective Jack Boyer e-mailed the news to Crystal Ferguson, thanking her for the vital part she had played in bringing him to justice. Since hearing her worst fears for Suzette realized, Crystal had been devastated and fallen into a deep depression.

"This has killed me inside," she said. "I have nightmares. I hear Suz's voice telling me to bring her home. I hear his voice telling me Suz was no good and he loves me. I may be a slave as Suz was but you do not hurt my baby without paying for it."

Aware of her fragile state, Detective Boyer urged her to be strong for Suzette and her family, warning that she may be called as a key witness at the upcoming preliminary hearing.

"The truth WILL come out in trial and Robinson will pay," he wrote her. "Let us continue working towards getting Robinson his punishment. You have been a great help to us and I know that this has been a very trying time for you. I know you are hurt and angry and I understand why.

"As our investigation has gone on I have had the opportunity to kind of get to know you. I very much sympathize with our loss."

Remembering an e-mail JT had once sent, saying he had removed all of Suzette's rings, Crystal had asked Boyer if they were there when her body was found. The detective assured her that all the piercing rings were intact, and so were the ones on her fingers.

"I thought it odd he didn't remove them to dispose of them," he wrote, "but let's face it, Robinson isn't real smart."

Soon after John Robinson was charged with multiple murder, his family released a second statement, attacking the press treatment of "our husband and father." It said the family was "devastated by the event," and that their thoughts were with the victims' friends and families.

"While we try to get through this situation day-by-day, we ask that we be allowed to put our lives back together in peace," it read. "Our ultimate goal is for the truth, no matter what that might be, to come to light."

The Robinson family then accused the press of undermining the legal process by "rumor and innuendo," saying that the proper place for evidence was in a courtroom.

"Healing must begin for everyone involved and it is time for investigators to be allowed to find the complete truth."

Amazingly, Robinson's daughter Christy Shipps apparently embarked on a clandestine public relations campaign in *The Kansas City Star*, on behalf of her father.

Immediately after Robinson's arrest the *Star* had placed an e-mail message board on its Website, for readers' feedback on the case. It soon generated hostile messages and discussion from many of the victims' friends and family under the mask of anonymity, hotly debating the murders and BDSM in general.

Christy, herself an emergency medical worker married to a Kansas detective, evidently soon felt she had to justify her father to her friends. She sent a cryptic e-mail to her old neighbor and school friend Hilary Adams, using the address, *mrsmedic@yahoo.com*. It read: "[My father] did not push any sickness on us. He was and is a loving and caring father and grandfather."

Adams, who now lived in Washington DC and hadn't seen Christy since their days at Blue Valley High School, was amazed when she received it out of the blue.

"It's very weird," said Adams. "I guess she feels she has to defend him in some way."

Then messages from *mrsmedic@yahoo.com* started appearing on the Talkback site. They complained bitterly about "vengeance" from the families of the victims, even advising them not to testify against John Robinson in court, as it would expose "deviate" BDSM details about their loved ones.

"I don't know if these victims were involved in the BDSM lifestyle," she wrote, "but if they were, do these families REALLY want everything about their activities discussed and opened to the world?"

In another Talkback e-mail addressed directly to Lisa Stasi's friend Kathy Rogers, the message took another tack, claiming that the Robinson family was just as victimized as anyone else.

"The public is very quick to judge people on half the story alone," the message stated. "No one knows the whole story—NOT even the families of the victims or his family. Is his family not victims in this? I think they are. If he did it or not he has rights too."

Replying to another Talkback e-mail from Suzette Trouten's sister Kim Padilla, *mrsmedic@yahoo.com* cryptically told her only to believe half of what she had been told by police about the Robinson case; a strange comment from a detective's wife.

"I understand that you have to be mad at someone," she wrote. "but don't you want the whole truth? If he did this then he deserves whatever he gets, but if he didn't he deserves to get on with his life. People need to remember that the U.S. has a constitution and everyone has rights under it."

Kim was terribly hurt by the e-mails questioning Christy's motives in even wondering if John Robinson was guilty.

"The man had five bodies in his possession," she replied. "Don't you hate it when someone puts dead bodies in your storage unit?"

On June 16, the Robinson Homicides Task Force announced that they were now investigating the 1994 disappearances of Sheila and Debbie Faith, raising the number of possible known victims to eleven. Detectives had discovered that the Faiths' monthly Social Security checks for $1,016 were still being delivered to "Jim Turner" at Robinson's Olathe post office box. They asked for the public's assistance in locating the troubled California mother and her wheelchair-bound daughter, but few expected them to turn up alive.

Later that day, John Robinson appeared in Johnson County Court and listened impassively as he was formally charged in the murders of Suzette Trouten and Izabela Lewicka, the aggravated kidnapping of Trouten and two counts of sexual battery and one of felony theft.

For this court appearance Robinson wore a smart blue business suit and tie and even smirked at the television cameras as he was led in. It was stunning footage that would be used again and again by television stations, during future coverage of the case.

As Kansas was seeking the death penalty, Robinson was being defended by a team of three attorneys from the Topeka-based Kansas Death Penalty Defense Unit, led by attorney Ron Evans. Robinson's sole comment during the hearing was answering "Yes" when Judge Earle Jones asked him if he understood the charges.

That week *Time* magazine ran an article on the mysterious John Robinson, saying that if he was found guilty he would be "the most prolific serial killer to strike this region in a decade."

"Robinson's camouflage of drab normality fell away last week," read the article by David Thigpen, "revealing what authorities say is a stealthy serial murderer with a taste for sadomasochistic internet sites."

The John Robinson case was fast becoming a media circus as television crews from *Dateline NBC* and ABC's *20/20*, descended on Olathe to research lengthy segments on the Robinson case, projected for airing during the November sweeps week. Sensing financial rewards, some of the victims' families hired lawyers to arrange lucrative exclusives for their personal stories.

Lisa Stasi's husband Carl, who had already been told that his daughter Tiffany had been adopted by Robinson's brother Donald and renamed, was awaiting the results of DNA tests on Heather Robinson, who was now fifteen years old and had just finished her freshman year at a public high school in Chicago. He hired a lawyer to arrange a reconciliation with Tiffany and negotiate film rights.

"It'd make a hell of a movie," Carl Stasi told one reporter, inviting him to make an offer. "I'd need a good price. You better get it now because they're starting to roll in. I got people overseas calling."

As yet Paul Morrison had managed to keep Tiffany's new identity secret, but he knew it was only a matter of time before it would go public, as he intended to call her as a witness when Robinson finally went on trial.

CHAPTER 24

THE POLITICS OF MURDER

A week later Sheila Faith was positively identified through dental records as one of the three bodies found in the storage locker in Raymore. Her disabled daughter Debbie would later be named as the final Jane Doe. Although detectives had now named all five bodies in the barrels, the murder investigation continued on both sides of the state line.

The Kansas Death Penalty Defense Unit was also busy preparing its case to save Robinson from death row, having just received the first installment of an epic nineteen-volume police report, laying out the case against Robinson.

Although a preliminary hearing had been set for the beginning of October in the Johnson County Courthouse, no one doubted that the defense would file motions to delay it well into 2001. And facing the prospect of not being able to try Robinson in Missouri for up to four years, Chris Koster was beginning to get impatient.

On Thursday, July 6, Cass County Circuit Judge William Collins, postponed preliminary motions in the Missouri case, as the defendant was in Kansas. Then without consulting Paul Morrison, Chris Koster told the Cass County *Democrat Missourian* that he was working on a plan to bring Robinson back and forth across state lines to attend future hearings.

"Missouri's ready to go," said Koster enthusiastically. "I believe we have everything needed to try this case."

When Morrison first heard about it from a reporter from *The Kansas City Star* he was livid, fearing his colleague's inexperience could jeopardize the whole case.

"My understanding is there are serious legal problems with bringing a prisoner back and forth over state lines," he told the *Star*, who ran a story of the "rift" between the two prosecutors. "We just can't control the variables, and it would be an understatement to say we would be playing with fire if we attempted any of that."

Chris Koster tried to defend himself, saying that if his case was put on hold for so long, witnesses' memories would fade and the evidence would be old.

A Kansas City attorney who specializes in extradition law said that Koster was "wet behind the ears," as Morrison would never let Robinson leave Kansas until after his trial there.

"There are too many potential problems of a defendant crossing state lines," he explained. "What you have here is an inexperienced prosecutor dreaming and losing his grip on reality. It's just so far off base."

A few days later an editorial in *The Kansas City Star* demanded that Kansas try Robinson before Missouri. It listed a number of reasons, including the fact that the first bodies were discovered in Kansas and Morrison had a proven track record, being widely regarded among his peers as a prosecutor's prosecutor.

"Koster's scheme to haul Robinson back and forth across the state line so Koster can score some prosecution points before Morrison should be halted in its tracks," declared the editorial.

Koster was forced to back down gracefully, resigning himself to sitting out the lengthy Kansas trial process before he could start his own. A few weeks later he would explain his frustrations, saying both sides want to see their cases move forward, but admitting that Kansas had the advantage as Robinson was in custody there.

On Friday, July 28, the case took an even stranger

twist when John Robinson was charged with the 1985
first-degree murder of Lisa Stasi, whose body had never
been found, and the aggravated interference with the parental custody of her daughter Tiffany, and concealment
of the child's whereabouts.

Just hours later Paul Morrison called a press conference in Overland Park to explain the delicate situation,
saying he was brokering a deal to reunite the girl, now
fifteen years old, with her biological family.

Although it was widely known among Kansas City
media that Robinson's brother Donald had unwittingly
raised the girl from infancy, Morrison still officially refused to reveal her identity. All he would say was that
she lived in the Midwest and that Robinson was well
known to the couple, who had paid him thousands of
dollars to cover what they believed to be a legal adoption.

"There is paperwork that would appear to be genuine
if you didn't know any better," Morrison explained at
the emotional press conference, attended by members of
Lisa Stasi's family.

FBI Special Agent Dirk Tarpley then read a dramatic
statement from Donald Robinson and his wife.

We too have been betrayed by [John Robinson]. We
have and will continue to cooperate with the authorities investigating the allegations surrounding John
Robinson.

We love our daughter very much. Since her adoption, which was never kept from her, we have always
assumed that as she became an adult, she would be
curious about her birth family. Because we were unaware whom her birth family was, it was our intention to assist her in any way possible in her efforts
in identifying and locating them. The circumstances

surrounding the investigation of John Robinson are
as distressing to our immediate family as they are to
the other families victimized. Our daughter is aware
of the investigation and we are doing our best to help
her through this difficult time.

Donald Robinson's family then appealed to the press
to respect their privacy, while they tried to come to terms
with the shocking truth. Carl Stasi did not attend, later
telling reporters in a telephone interview that it was the
best news he'd had since his wife had disappeared. The
following week his attorney began negotiations with
ABC's *20/20* and the tabloid television show *Inside Edition*, for a proposed segment about him being reunited
with his daughter.

A month later Paul Morrison released a witness list
containing five hundred names of possible witnesses for
the upcoming preliminary hearing. Among them was
"Tiffany Stasi a.k.a. Heather Robinson." The media now
ran with the story that the unfortunate girl had been
raised by Robinson's younger brother. *The Kansas City
Star* even printed Heather's 2000 yearbook photograph
on its front page, prompting thirty readers to complain.

"We certainly feel bad for the girl," explained the
Star's editor Mark Zieman in an editorial. "We always
have to balance an individual's privacy with the public's
right to know. In this case we sided with the girl until
her identity became public locally. I thought the photo
and name went together."

Even John Robinson's daughter Christy, who had
grown up believing that Heather was her cousin, at-
tacked the *Star* in its own Talkback message board.

"What this paper did to her was one of the worst
crimes I have ever seen," she wrote on August 26. "How

dare they print her picture, she is a minor. People have NO compassion in the world at all."

In mid-August, D.A. Paul Morrison brokered a deal between Carl Stasi and Donald Robinson, so Stasi could eventually meet his daughter. Saying that he had no problems with her adoptive parents and would not seek custody, Stasi agreed to take a DNA test to confirm he was her biological father. If the tests proved positive, the long process of getting to know his daughter would begin, under the close supervision of psychologists.

On Thursday, August 31, John Robinson was back in Johnson County District Court, where his lawyers won a six-week delay for the preliminary hearing. Robinson's lawyer from the Kansas Death Penalty Defense Unit, Ron Evans, said he needed more time to review the thirteen thousand pages of prosecution evidence. The immaculately tailored Robinson remained silent throughout the hearing, which was postponed until November 13.

Two months later Evans won another reprieve for Robinson when Judge John Anderson III delayed the preliminary hearing until February 5, 2001. But he said it would take an "extraordinary event indeed" for him to push it back any further.

When asked by Judge Anderson if he understood the reason for delaying his preliminary hearing, John Robinson answered: "Yes, Your Honor, so my attorneys can be prepared."

Later D.A. Paul Morrison said the investigation was continuing and there would be further police reports right up to the day of Robinson's trial.

That fall, before leaving on a well-deserved vacation, Detective Jack Boyer sent Crystal a final e-mail, urging her to be careful in the BDSM lifestyle. Earlier he had angered her by requesting her computer hard drive as evidence. Crystal had refused, explaining that every time she turned on her computer, Suzette's ICQ name and number still appeared on the screen. It was her last link to her dead soulmate and one she refused to relinquish under any circumstances.

"Suzette cannot reauthorize," said Crystal, close to tears. "I can be typing for three hours and all I've got to do is look down at her name and she's with me. I can replace everything on there except for her."

She also told the detective that she was now seriously considering getting out of the BDSM lifestyle after what had happened to Suzette.

"How can I allow myself to be blindfolded again?" she asked. "Knowing it's when I'm most vulnerable."

The detective, who had grown close to Crystal, although they had never met, offered this advice: "There may or may not be more persons like Robinson out there, so if you were to ask my opinion, I would tell you to be careful and follow your instincts.

"Like I said at the beginning, I am not here to judge what people do in the confines of their own homes. But, if you come out to play and a crime is committed be prepared to either pay the piper or the consequences."

EPILOGUE

On Monday, February 5, 2001, John Robinson was led into the modern stone-and-red-brick Johnson County District Court for his long-awaited preliminary hearing. Wearing a smart business suit and clutching a yellow legal pad, Robinson could easily have passed as a lawyer, as he traded quips with his legal team, headed up by Ron Evans of Kansas' Death Penalty Defense Unit.

A month earlier Cass County Prosecutor Chris Koster had introduced yet another dimension to the complex Robinson case by adding fifty-six fraud and forgery charges to the three murder charges already brought by Missouri.

"I don't think that someone accused of a homicide deserves the benefit of the state backing off," declared the prosecutor, adding that Beverly Bonner and the Faiths had been killed for financial gain.

The new charges alleged that between 1994 and 1997 Robinson had defrauded the US government of more than $29,000 in Social Security and disability payments by forging documents maintaining that Sheila and Debbie Faith were still alive. Koster also charged that between February 1994 and June 1995 Robinson stole more than 14,000 dollars' worth of Bonner's alimony checks.

The two counts of fraud and fifty-four forgery charges each carried a maximum seven-year prison sentence. Robinson now faced up to 382 years in a Missouri prison if found guilty on all of them; that is, if he managed to dodge the death penalty Koster was demanding in the other three murder cases.

But even with the combined power of the Missouri and Kansas judicial systems bearing down upon him, John Robinson didn't look the least concerned as he entered Johnson County District Court. The preliminary hearing, already twice postponed at the defense's request, would decide if there was enough evidence to bind Robinson over for trial. And during the next five days Veteran Judge John Anderson III would hear damning testimony from more than fifty prosecution witnesses, including Robinson's wife Nancy and brother Donald.

Ironically, although it was billed as the most eagerly awaited murder trial in Kansas City for years, and Johnson County Courthouse had heightened its security, introducing an elaborate pass system for the media and members of the public, only a handful of print journalists, radio reporters and television crews bothered to attend. The third-floor media room, which had been especially equipped with closed-circuit television sets and extra phone lines, was relatively quiet.

Judge Anderson's gleaming wood-paneled Court Sixteen on the fourth floor holds sixty people in three rows of plush, comfortable seating. And by 9:00 a.m. on Monday morning they were full up with several of the victims' families sitting across from members of the Robinson clan.

Emotions on both sides were running high when John Robinson suddenly appeared from behind the jury box and sat down between his legal team of Ron Evans and Mark Manna from the Topeka-based Death Penalty Defense Unit and defense attorney Alice Craig White. For the next five days Robinson would sit impassively as Paul Morrison and his Assistant District

Attorney Sara Welch, presented their voluminous case against him.

Robinson now faced capital murder charges of killing Suzette Trouten and Izabela Lewicka, the first-degree murder of Lisa Stasi, aggravated interference with the parental custody of Tiffany Stasi, aggravated kidnapping of Suzette Trouten, two charges of aggravated sexual battery of Melissa Wright and Virginia Dickson and the felony theft of Dickson's sex toys.

The first prosecution witness to be called by Paul Morrison was Crystal Ferguson, who had flown in from Canada the previous Saturday. It had been a very emotional time for Crystal, who had spent Sunday with Suzette's mother Carolyn Trouten and visited the grave of her murdered lover.

Crystal had long dreaded taking the stand and seeing John Robinson face to face for the first time. But when she actually set eyes on him, she felt "absolutely nothing."

"He stared at me the whole time and wrote on his little pad," said Crystal a few days later. "I felt cold."

During her hour-long testimony, Crystal told Judge Anderson how she had first met Suzette in an S&M chat room and how their relationship had developed through their shared interest in bondage and domination. Then she candidly described how it had evolved into something deeper during her two visits to see Suzette in Michigan.

In a hushed voice, she remembered Suzette's sudden announcement that she was moving to Kansas to care for the elderly father of a wealthy man. Crystal said she had warned her friend that there was something fishy about the $65,000-a-year job and the exotic travel involved, but Suzette refused to listen.

Then she told the court about their last ICQ contact

on the morning of Suzette's disappearance and how she had started receiving e-mails from the mysterious J. R. soon afterwards. Robinson began taking careful notes as Crystal told how she had become suspicious after receiving a flood of uncharacteristic e-mails purporting to come from Suzette, and how she had worked with detectives to gather evidence against Robinson.

The next witness was Carolyn Trouten, who described her youngest child as "kind of a mama's girl."

In emotional testimony she told of her final phone call to a "happy" Suzette, a few minutes before Robinson arrived at her hotel room on March 1.

"She told me she wasn't as homesick as she thought she would be," said Trouten.

The judge then heard how members of Suzette's family began receiving suspicious e-mails, which she immediately knew weren't from her daughter, because of the uncharacteristically perfect spelling and punctuation.

"That wasn't Suzy," said Trouten. "It just wasn't her."

With tears in her eyes she then described calling the Olathe telephone number Suzette had left and how Robinson had answered the phone, saying that her daughter had run off with a man named Jim Turner.

After completing her emotional testimony Carolyn Trouten was interviewed outside the court by the local NBC affiliate KSHB-TV. Asked if she thought Robinson had killed Suzette she replied, "Absolutely." But apparently unable to come to terms with her daughter's fascination with bondage, Carolyn still maintained that Suzette's "alternative lifestyle" had not contributed to her death.

On Tuesday morning Nancy Robinson arrived at court to make her first public appearance since her husband's arrest nine months earlier. With a hat shielding her face from the TV cameramen and press photogra-

phers on the courtroom steps, she was escorted inside
by her daughter Christy and family attorney Thomas
Kelly Ryan.

As she entered the courtroom to take the stand as a
prosecution witness, she seemed composed, staring
blankly at the man she had been married to for almost
four decades.

Before she was sworn in, Judge Anderson ordered the
court TV cameras to be turned off and then advised her
of her rights to take the Fifth Amendment and not risk
incriminating herself by testifying against her husband.
After a short conference with Ryan, Nancy returned to
the witness stand and began her damning testimony.

The whole court seemed to hold its breath as Nancy
cast her mind back sixteen years to the freezing January day when her husband arrived home holding little
Tiffany Stasi in his arms, straight after he allegedly
murdered her mother Lisa. Nancy remembered there
was a heavy snowstorm and the toddler was "physically dirty."

"He was alone when he came in with the baby,"
Nancy told District Attorney Paul Morrison, as John
Robinson stared ahead impassively.

She explained that as her husband had not brought
any extra baby clothes, diapers or formula, she had gone
out to buy some, as soon as the snow stopped. She then
identified a photograph of Tiffany as the same baby her
husband had brought home, sadly informing the court
that she and Robinson would celebrate their thirty-
seventh wedding anniversary in April.

The following morning her brother-in-law Donald and
his wife had flown into Kansas City from Chicago to
collect Tiffany, whom they believed they were legally
adopting. After spending the night and posing for a family photograph, with John Robinson holding up the little

baby girl, they left to return to Chicago with the infant
they had renamed Heather Tiffany Robinson.

At the end of her testimony Nancy Robinson took a
seat next to her daughter Christy and other members of
the Robinson family, just a few feet behind her husband.
For the rest of the day they listened to compelling evidence from a series of detectives and forensic patholo-
gists about the grisly findings in John Robinson's Olathe
storage locker and on his Kansas farm.

Lenexa Detectives Dawn Layman and Dan Owsley
told how they went to Robinson's Locker B-18 at Needmor Storage on the afternoon of his arrest. Inside they
found personal items belonging to Suzette Trouten and
Izabela Lewicka, including a birth certificate, driver's
license, Social Security card, a passport application and
two slave contracts bearing each of the victims' names.

The two detectives showed Judge Anderson a stack
of stationery signed by Trouten and Lewicka as well as
empty envelopes addressed to their close family and
friends.

"Some of them say, 'Love ya, Suzette,' " explained
Detective Layman, who added there were "some varia-
tions in the package."

Next on the witness stand was stand was Detective
Harold Hughes of the Johnson County Sheriff's Department who was the first person to open the two oil barrels
found on Saturday, June 3, at Robinson's Linn County
farm. In grisly testimony Hughes told the court how the
remains of Suzette Trouten and Izabela Lewicka were
both lying face-down in a fetal position. The bodies were
naked and blindfolded, with ropes around their necks.

Deputy Shawnee County Coroner Donald Pojman,
who performed autopsies the following day in Topeka,
said both women had died from heavy blows to the left
side of the head, made with enough force to puncture

holes in the skulls. He speculated that they had been caused by the head of a hammer although under defense cross-examination he admitted they could have been caused by any round object.

The third day of the preliminary hearing concentrated on Izabela Lewicka, who had moved to Kansas City to be near John Robinson in summer 1997, after meeting him over the Internet. John Robinson took notes as the court heard that the pretty Polish-born nineteen-year-old from West Lafayette, Indiana, had begun calling herself "Mrs. Robinson" a few months after arriving.

Her father, Andrzei Lewicki, a physics lab coordinator at Purdue University, said Izabela had just completed her freshman year at Purdue University when she suddenly announced she was moving to Kansas, to take up an internship. After she left the only contact he and his wife had with her was through e-mails. Lewicki said his daughter had mentioned that she had gotten married but refused to give any details about her husband. All she would tell her parents was that she was doing fine and spending a lot of time abroad.

In the two years Izabela lived in Kansas, until her disappearance in the fall of 1999, John Robinson rented several apartments for her. A printer named Karen Scott testified that Robinson had introduced her to Izabela sometime in 1998, saying that she was a graphic designer for one of his modular home magazines.

Scott said that in September 1999 Robinson had asked if she could recommend a Web designer for a new magazine of his. When Scott questioned why Izabela couldn't do the work, Robinson explained that she had recently been deported after being caught smoking marijuana.

"I didn't understand what happened to her," Scott told the court.

The next witness was a young Kansas City woman named Celia Crosby (not her real name) who said Robinson had answered a personal advertisement she had placed in *Pitch Weekly* in late 1997, offering a mature man sex in return for financial compensation. In a hushed voice Crosby told how Robinson had agreed to pay the rent on her Kansas City apartment and $2,000 a month, in exchange for sexual favors.

"I was to be available for him whenever he wanted," said Crosby, who added that Robinson only ever gave her small amounts of cash, although she continued having sex with him for over two years, even signing a slave contract.

In the fall of 1999 Robinson proposed marriage, giving her a gold band which looked "used." He also offered her a highly paid job as his personal assistant, promising extensive travel to Europe and Australia. Initially she agreed to both offers, but grew suspicious when Robinson asked her to write letters to her family, to be sent later while they were abroad. When she asked why, Robinson had explained she would be far too busy traveling to write letters so it was prudent to do it in advance.

Ultimately Crosby ended the relationship, telling Robinson she didn't want anything further to do with him. He then lashed out in revenge, sending her mother sexually explicit photographs he had taken of her during their relationship.

Next on the witness stand was Mary White, the middle-aged Canadian woman, who had known John Robinson since he was a teenager. She told the court how they had met almost forty years earlier when he was visiting Canada on a musical tour. She said they had struck up a friendship and become pen pals. After marrying Nancy Jo, he had visited her in Canada in the early 1970s, never mentioning that he was already married with children.

It would be another twenty years before Mary heard from him again. She said that in 1993 her parents had received a letter, purporting to come from one of John Robinson's sons. It stated that Robinson had remained a bachelor and had adopted the children of his brother, who had been tragically killed in a crash. The letter said that after all this time his father still thought about her.

Now living in England and on her third husband, White eagerly replied to the letter, re-igniting their relationship. Over the next six years they regularly spoke on the telephone and corresponded by e-mail. She was much impressed when Robinson told her he was a successful businessman who secretly worked for the CIA on top-secret assignments. When she separated from her husband in June 1999, Robinson invited her to move to Kansas City to be near him, and she had agreed.

"I was just happy to be in the same town," she said.

Initially Robinson checked her into a suite at a Lenexa extended stay hotel on his MasterCard. A few weeks later he moved her into the same furnished apartment in Overland Park where Izabela Lewicka had lived.

During the nine months she lived at the duplex Robinson would only come around twice a week and the occasional weekend, saying he was working all the time. But White told the court that even though she rarely saw him she had believed they had a future together.

In May 2000, White had returned to Canada to look after her aging parents. The plan was for Robinson to follow at the end of June. Then they would set up home together. But while she was preparing for his arrival, Lenexa detectives telephoned with the news that he had been arrested as an alleged serial murderer.

Later, when detectives searched the Overland Park

duplex where she had lived, they found the bed made up with the same patterned green-diamond sheets that Izabela Lewicka's mother Danuta had earlier testified she had bought for her daughter. It was the same distinctive pillow-case material discovered with Izabela's body in the barrel.

Thursday, February 8, was an unusually warm winter's day in Kansas, with temperatures nearly hitting 60 degrees. There was almost a balmy mood in the courthouse as the television crews and print reporters arrived for the fourth and penultimate day of the preliminary hearing.

Today the prosecution planned to concentrate on Lisa and Tiffany Stasi. And although Tiffany, under her new name of Heather Robinson, was on the list of prosecution witnesses, few expected Morrison to call her.

First on the stand that morning was Tiffany's father Carl Stasi, who told the court how he had married Lisa in August 1984, when she was pregnant with his child. A month later he had been at her side when she gave birth.

The couple had separated soon afterwards, and in an effort to save the marriage, Stasi claimed, he had enlisted in the US Navy, so he could support his wife and baby.

"I told her wait and see where I get stationed and we'll try to work things out at that time," Stasi said. "It was looking good as long as I got a job."

Stasi left Kansas the day after Christmas 1984 for his first naval assignment and Lisa moved into a battered women's shelter. It was just a week later that social service workers unwittingly introduced her to John Robinson, under his alias, John Osborne.

Next on the stand was Lisa's sister-in-law, Kathy Klinginsmith, who was the last person to see her alive In emotional testimony she described how Robinson had arrived at her house in early January 1983, during a heavy snowstorm, and collected Lisa and Tiffany.

"I just remember I was so frightened," said Klinginsmith. "I wanted to run after her but I was too scared."

Asked by Morrison to identify the man Lisa had introduced her to as "John Osborne," Klinginsmith looked straight at Robinson, replying: "Well, yeah, he looks older, but he still looks evil."

The next witness was John Robinson's brother Donald, who, with his wife, had adopted little Tiffany, raising her in Chicago completely unaware that the adoption had been illegal, or of the terrible circumstances behind it.

Donald Robinson told the court how he and his wife were unable to have children because of health reasons and had read a magazine article about adoption opportunities in other states. When he raised the subject at a 1983 family reunion in Stanley, Kansas, John Robinson had immediately volunteered his services, saying he knew of an attorney who specialized in adoptions.

Donald told the court how he had paid his brother a total of $5,500 to cover legal costs and that he had completely trusted him. He explained how over the next couple of years his brother acted as "a go-between" for him and the lawyer, named Doug Wood. After several false alarms, Robinson called in January 1985 saying he had found a child, whose mother had recently committed suicide in a hotel.

On January 11, the day after Lisa and Tiffany Stasi disappeared, Donald and John Robinson flew into Kansas. Donald paid his brother $3,000 and they collected Tiffany, then returned to Chicago with the baby to start a new life.

Donald told Judge Anderson how they had given their new daughter the middle name Tiffany, as John Robinson had suggested that it was what her dead mother would have wanted.

A major snowstorm hit Kansas City early Friday morning, sending temperatures plummeting thirty degrees into the teens and closing local schools. Traffic edged along Sante Fe from I-35 to N. Kansas and there was a white blanket of snow shrouding the clock tower and the square in front of the courthouse.

The fifth and final day of the preliminary hearing saw Melissa Wright and Virginia Dickson testify how, in spring 2000, John Robinson had answered their personal ads on bondage and discipline Internet sites. The women, who both coincidentally came from Texas, had then embarked on e-mail relationships with Robinson, believing him to be a wealthy businessman. Finally they had both agreed to fly to Kansas City to meet him for sexual encounters.

Melissa Wright, a board-certified psychologist, described how she had arrived on Easter Sunday, checking into the Extended Stay America motel in Overland Park, where Robinson had made reservations. She said that soon after his arrival he had presented her with a slave contract, which she had duly signed.

"[I was] to give my body to him in any way he sees fit," Wright told Judge Anderson, adding that she had brought an array of sexual devices with her for the encounter. "He wanted me to say that I would be his slave, his slut, his whore."

Wright, who had been promised a new job by Robinson, soon discovered that her benefactor practiced far more extreme types of bondage than she was used to. Initially she had complied with his demands, as she wanted a job, but when he began shooting photographs of her engaged in oral sex, she had told him to stop.

Robinson had replied by slapping her hard in the face.

Then he ordered her to return to Dallas, pack up her things and prepare to move to Kansas, promising to support her until she found work. But once back in Texas, Robinson refused to take her telephone calls. When she asked him to return her 700 dollars' worth of sex toys, he'd refused, threatening to expose her as a deviant and ruin her career as a psychologist. Wright then got scared and called the police.

The final witness was Virginia Dickson, an accountant from Galveston, Texas. She told the hearing how she had traveled to Kansas City in mid-May, checking into the same Overland Park motel that Wright had, as instructed by Robinson.

It wasn't long before she realized that she was out of her league with Robinson, who demanded rough sex. A few days after she arrived, Robinson took pictures of her bound and gagged on the motel bed. When she tried to protest he flogged her and then ordered her to leave. After he abandoned her with no money outside the motel, she tearfully called the Lenexa police, who spent two days debriefing her in a nearby safe house.

Late Friday afternoon Judge Anderson recessed the preliminary hearing until March 2, saying he would then rule on whether there was enough evidence for Robinson to stand trial.

On February 19 John Robinson's lawyers filed a thirty-four-page motion saying Johnson County prosecutors could not try Robinson for multiple capital murders, as they didn't have the jurisdiction or enough evidence. Seeking a highly tentative legal loophole, which could set a precedent in future Kansas death penalty cases, Ron Evans argued that, as the state had tied the deaths of Suzette Trouten and Izabela Lewicka to three other women in Missouri, that evidence could not be used to support the Kansas charges, as they happened out-of-state. The defense also maintained that, as Lisa Stasi was allegedly murdered nine years before the Kansas death penalty law was enacted, Robinson could not be tried on capital murder charges.

"The state did not establish at the preliminary hearing that Lisa Stasi is deceased," stated the defense motion.

A week later District Attorney Paul Morrison filed his own twenty-page motion to support the charges. Claiming that the killings were part of a "common scheme or course of action," he wrote that to deny this would mean that "the State of Kansas meant to exclude serial killers from the capital murder statute."

"A murderer should not escape punishment because the exact place of his crime is concealed," said the motion.

On March 2, 2001, Judge Anderson ruled that John Robinson would have to stand trial for seven felony charges including the three capital murder charges of Suzette Trouten, Izabela Lewicka and Lisa Stasi. The only charge he dismissed was the sexual battery one, involving Virginia Dickson.

Straight after the ruling Paul Morrison handed defense lead attorney Ron Evans written notice that he would be seeking the death penalty if Robinson were to be convicted at his trial, expected later this year. Evans replied by saying his client would "stand silent" to all charges, prompting the judge to enter a not guilty plea on Robinson's behalf.

If a jury does convict John Robinson of murder he could become the first person to be executed in Kansas since 1965, the same year he first stepped outside the law.

* * *

On October 7, 2002, John Robinson was led into a Kansas courtroom, charged with the capital murders of Suzette Trouten, Izabela Lewicka and Lisa Stasi, as well as with arranging the fraudulent adoption of her baby Tiffany. And prosecutor Paul Morrison was demanding the death penalty.

Robinson, now 58, was once again playing fast and loose with the Kansas court system. Fifteen months earlier he had sacked his defense team, hiring a recent law school graduate named Bob Thomas, who had only been practicing law for a year. Savvy Johnson County Prosecutor Paul Morrison, realizing how the young attorney's inexperience would be grounds for a later appeal, persuaded Judge John Anderson III to appoint two highly experienced Missouri-based death penalty attorneys to assist the defense, thus thwarting Robinson.

In his opening statements, Morrison took the jury back seventeen years, to when John Robinson had collected Lisa Stasi and Tiffany from Kathy Klinginsmith, during a snowstorm. Then, after killing Lisa, he had handed over the baby to his unwitting brother, Don, and his wife, who had flown in from Chicago.

"They raised the baby as their own," Morrison told the jury.

He then explained how the Internet's first serial killer had been caught after Suzette Trouten's disappearance in March 2000, leading to a massive police investigation.

Eventually Trouten's and Lewicka's bodies had been discovered in barrels on his Kansas farm. The bodies of his other three victims were found several days later in his storage locker in Raymore, Missouri.

The trial captured national attention with all its sensational elements of sadomasochistic sex, the dangers of the Internet and cold-blooded murder. And over the

three-week trial the six-man, six-woman jury heard testimony from 110 witnesses and were shown 500 exhib-
its, including an array of esoteric sexual devices, X-rated
photographs and videos, demonstrating the grandfather's
obsession with kinky sex. Robinson's wife, Nancy, and
daughter, Christy, both attended the trial, taking the
stand to defend him and tell the jury how he was a dot-
ing, devoted grandfather. Nancy agreed she was aware
of her husband's infidelities, and would have divorced
him if it hadn't been for their children. But she denied
knowing anything about his murderous double-life.

His brother, Don Robinson, also testified about how
he had delivered Tiffany to him to adopt, after claiming
her mother had recently committed suicide.

Ultimately it took the jury eleven hours to reach a
guilty verdict on all counts. And John Robinson, who
had never taken the stand in his own defense, sat impassively without a flicker of emotion as the verdicts
were read.

Three days later the jury reconvened for the death
penalty phase of the trial, which began on Halloween.
Dramatically taking the stand to plead for her husband's
life, Nancy Robinson tearfully recounted a jailhouse visit
her husband had had with his eight-year-old granddaughter soon after his arrest.

She described how she and their daughter, Christy
had waited in the lobby as a guard escorted the little gir
to see her grandfather, who was wearing an orange
prison suit, in his cell.

"Papa, orange is not your color," declared the little
girl, throwing her arms around him.

On hearing this John Robinson slowly removed hi
glasses and began to cry. It was his first display of an
emotion since his arrest.

"It's devastating," Nancy sobbed, begging the jury to save his life. "He's their dad. He's their grandfather. They love him."

But Prosecutor Morrison, calling Robinson the 'infidel deluxe,' countered by accusing the defendant of actually taking his granddaughter along to several of his sordid S & M sex sessions.

Later when the jurors' unanimous decision that John Robinson should die for his terrible crimes was read out in court, none of his family were there to hear Judge Anderson sentence him to death.

Now finally it was Missouri's turn to deal with John Robinson, but another trial was averted after Cass County Missouri Prosecutor Chris Koster made a controversial deal with the defense. The prosecutor agreed not to seek the death penalty in return for Robinson clearing up the mystery of what had happened to Paula Godfrey and Catherine Clampitt.

And in October 2003, John Robinson pleaded guilty to murdering Sheila Faith, her daughter Debbie, and Beverly Bonner.

"This was classic John Robinson," Kansas Prosecutor Paul Morrison commented, when told about the deal. "The guy was a gamesman to the end."

Now Robinson waits on death row in Kansas, as the automatic process to appeal his death sentence goes forward.